THE ART OF
RAW DESSERTS

THE ART OF
RAW DESSERTS

50 Standout Recipes for Plant-Based Cakes, Pastries,
Pies, Cookies and More

CRYSTAL BONNET
Creator of Crystal Dawn Culinary

PAGE STREET
PUBLISHING CO.

PAGE STREET
PUBLISHING CO.

This book is for everyone who has supported me
during my journey and trusted me to teach you.
This book would not be possible without you all.

TABLE OF CONTENTS

Introduction ... 9

The Foundations of Creating Raw Desserts ... 11
What Is Considered Raw? ... 12
Equipment and Tools for the Raw Kitchen ... 13
Getting Familiar with Your Ingredients ... 14
Prep Notes ... 18
Powdered Pantry Staples ... 18
Processing Crusts and Batters ... 19
Blending ... 19
Melting/Liquefying ... 19
Activating Nuts and Seeds ... 20
Troubleshooting Chocolate ... 21

The Building-Block Recipes ... 23
Almond Milk ... 24
Brazil Nut Milk ... 25
Hazelnut Milk ... 25
Pistachio Milk ... 26
Pecan Milk ... 26
Coconut Milk ... 27
Coconut Cream ... 27
Activated Oat Flour ... 28
Sprouted and Dehydrated Buckwheat ... 29
Cultured Cashew Filling ... 30
Coconut Butter ... 31
Agar Paste ... 31

Heavenly Chocolate and Truffles ... 33

White Chocolate Peppermint Fudge ... 34
Orange Hazelnut Fudge ... 37
Milk Chocolate Cherry Cinnamon Truffles ... 40
Lavender Berry White Chocolate Truffles ... 43
Buckwheat Crunch Chocolate Bars with Apricot Jam ... 44
Mexican Chocolate Mousse Bars ... 47

Delectable Cakes ... 51

Strawberry Vanilla Cheesecake ... 52
Raspberry White Chocolate Cheesecake ... 55
Apple Crumble Caramel Cheesecake ... 58
Blackberry Ginger Lime Zebra Cheesecake ... 61
Mocha Crisp Cheesecake ... 64
Chocolate Mousse Cake with Cherry Jam ... 67
Tropical Lime Coconut Entremets ... 69
Apricot Pecan Butternut Squash Cake with Coconut Cream ... 73
Carrot Cake with Orange Cheesecake Frosting ... 76
Three-Layer Tiramisu Cake ... 81

Perfect Pastries and Cookies ... 85

Lemon Poppy Seed Coconut Shortbread Cookies ... 86
Matcha Raspberry Linzer Cookies ... 89
Mocha Donuts with Espresso Glaze ... 92
Almond Fig and Cardamom Cookie Sandwiches ... 95
Mango Berry Crêpes with Coconut Cream ... 98

Healthier Pies and Tarts ... 101

Chocolate Mint Cream Tarts ... 102
Chocolate Hazelnut Praline Tarts ... 105
Pecan Pie with Rosemary and Orange ... 107
Raspberry Beet Mousse and Carob Tarts ... 111
Avocado Key Lime Pies with Coconut Cream ... 112
Banana Cream Pie with Gingerbread Crust ... 115

Creamy Ice Cream without the Dairy ... 119

Vanilla Bean Ice Cream ... 120
Mint Chocolate Chip Ice Cream ... 123
Decadent Chocolate Ice Cream ... 124
Berries and Cream Coconut Ice-Cream Cake ... 127
Chocolate Chip Ice-Cream Cookie Sandwiches ... 130

Delightful Slices and Bars ... 133

Tiger Nut Tahini Slice ... 134
Double Chocolate Red Velvet Brownies ... 137
Strawberry Rose Pistachio Cream Slice ... 140
Hawaiian Sunshine Crumble Squares ... 143

Raw Frostings, Garnishes and Finishing Touches ... 147

Coconut Frosting ... 148
Rich Vanilla Cream Frosting ... 149
Double Chocolate Frosting ... 150
Cultured Cashew Frosting Base ... 151
Candied Cacao Nibs ... 152
Dark Chocolate Ganache ... 153
Chocolate Sauce ... 154
Enrobing Dark Chocolate ... 156
Vanilla Bean Coconut Whip ... 157
White Chocolate Sauce ... 158
Ginger Caramel Sauce ... 159

Substitutions List ... 160
Acknowledgments ... 161
About the Author ... 162
Index ... 163

INTRODUCTION

Welcome to my world of raw desserts; I'm so happy you've decided to pick up this book and learn my methods for creating not only delicious and nutritious sweets, but ones that look stunning and will impress anyone. Whether you're an at-home cook or a professional with experience making raw desserts, there are recipes in this cookbook for everyone's skill level.

All the recipes in this book are no-bake, made without any dairy, eggs, gluten, soy, corn or refined sugar. Not only are they free of most common allergens, but raw desserts are also packed full of nutrition, less processed and sometimes diabetic friendly, making them a much healthier alternative to traditional sweets and desserts. We cover all bases of raw desserts, from pantry staple replacements to layered cakes to ice cream and every sweet treat in between.

My raw dessert journey began when I decided to upgrade my diet to incorporate plant-based, raw, whole, living foods. I adopted this way of eating to better my health, clear my skin and, overall, just feel better. I was always interested in health but was not an avid cook, so I ate processed, unhealthy foods until my early adult life—and I started developing health issues, such as cystic acne, chronic fatigue, depression and a weak immune system. When I learned about raw food (we dive more into what raw food actually is in the next chapter), I was fascinated and fell in love with the creativity of raw food cooking; this is where I truly found my passion. Raw food and desserts are creative, vibrant and make you feel good.

I learned everything I could about raw food and stumbled across raw chocolate making. I was amazed by all the delicious raw, vegan chocolate and desserts that are available. I've always had a love affair with chocolate, so once I found out I could enjoy healthier versions, I was obsessed! This obsession led me to sell my raw chocolate and dessert creations at farmers markets and eventually educate others on making their own at home.

Raw desserts have advanced exponentially since they exploded on the vegan scene. Many excellent tools and pieces of equipment are available to achieve those familiar textures we are used to in traditional, baked desserts. My favorite and must-have kitchen appliances for raw dessert making are a high-speed blender, such as a Vitamix®, a food processor and a food dehydrator. There is more information about tools and equipment on page 13.

Desserts are an excellent introduction to vegan food, so my approach to raw dessert making is to win over anyone and hopefully persuade them to eat more foods without animal products. I focus not only on taste but also aesthetics by making them even better than the traditional, baked versions. Most of these recipes have been tested on nonvegan skeptics; they have loved all the recipes and keep asking for more! That is how I know anyone will love these desserts.

My ultimate goal as a teacher is for you to succeed. I have included all my chef tips and tricks in this book to contribute to your raw dessert–making success. I hope you enjoy these recipes as much as I do!

Happy "Unbaking!"

Crystal Bonnet

THE FOUNDATIONS
OF CREATING
RAW DESSERTS

This chapter is probably the most crucial chapter in this
book. I dive into essential notes about what is considered
raw, introduce raw ingredients you will be working with
and show you how to work with them. Tips are provided
on sourcing your ingredients to help you save money
and I recommend suppliers so you know where to source
ingredients in bulk. I also included instructions on storing
your ingredients properly to maintain freshness
and longevity.

Then, we dive into prepping your raw ingredients and
important techniques in raw dessert making, such as
processing crusts, melting and liquefying, blending and
even troubleshooting chocolate. I'm excited for
you to get started!

WHAT IS CONSIDERED RAW?

Raw food has many different definitions and variations. When we refer to raw desserts in this book, we refer to vegan, plant-based, gluten-free, whole food prepared under a temperature of 114 to 118°F (46 to 48°C). Studies have shown that heating food above 118°F (48°C) destroys or degrades living nutrients, such as vitamins, minerals and antioxidants. Raw desserts are generally healthier because they do not contain animal products, refined sugars or gluten, making them an excellent option for people with allergies.

It is essential to understand that many ingredients used in raw foods and desserts are not actually raw, since they are heated over 118°F (48°C) before you buy them. Unless you're making a dessert with only fruits, coconut or nuts and seeds, almost 100 percent of the time the recipe includes an ingredient that is not considered raw. You have to decide what "raw" means to you. If I'm making a cake that is not baked and involves processing, blending, dehydrating and using unrefined, vegan and predominantly raw ingredients, I will call it a raw vegan cake. Let's go over some of the most common ingredients we will be using.

Almonds

Almonds grown in the U.S. are steam treated and therefore not considered raw; if you want to source genuinely raw almonds, source ones from Europe; they are usually called "European almonds," grown in Italy or Spain.

Cashews

Native to India, cashews are one of the most widely used nuts in raw cuisine because they are one of the best alternatives to dairy for creating a creamy consistency. We use cashews for cheesecakes, ice creams, cakes and frostings. Cashews are not actually a nut; they are a seed that grows on the outside of a cashew apple in a toxic shell that contains a resin called urushiol, which is also the same toxin in poison ivy. Because of this toxin, the shells are removed using a steaming process and most of the time, they are further roasted to ensure any traces of urushiol are removed. There are genuinely raw cashews available that have been manually removed from the shell, but the workers removing them suffer from severe burns and rashes. Do your research before sourcing genuinely raw cashews.

Cacao

Another widely used ingredient that is not actually raw is cacao. Cacao is made from the seeds of the cacao fruit. The seeds are removed, fermented and dried, creating cacao nibs, and further processed to create cacao butter, cacao paste and cacao powder. It's important to understand the difference between cocoa and cacao. Cocoa products are made from roasted cocoa beans, whereas cacao products are made from unroasted cacao beans. You can tell the difference in appearance and taste; cacao powder is lighter in color, generally sweeter and higher in magnesium and iron.

It is difficult to source truly raw cacao because, during fermentation and processing, there is a high probability that temperatures reach well and above the 118°F (48°C) "raw" threshold. These processes are generally not regulated in the countries where they are produced, so you never really know. There is much debate on this subject in the raw community, but I would rather be more conscious of sourcing fair-trade, organic, non-GMO cacao products than worry so much about the temperature it was processed at. Chocolate is very nutritious, and I don't know about you, but I cannot go a day without it!

Sweeteners

The dry and liquid sweeteners in these recipes include coconut sugar, maple syrup, agave, coconut nectar and sugar alcohols. Although they are still processed in some way and heated, in my opinion, these sweeteners are a much healthier option than traditional sugars used in baking since most of them are rich in minerals and other nutrients, and some are low glycemic.

Nut and Seed Butters

Sometimes I prefer to use a roasted nut or seed butter, such as tahini, because I prefer the flavor of roasted over raw. Anywhere I've used tahini in the recipes in the book, I always use roasted, but you have the option of using raw. I use raw almond butter, but you also have the option to use roasted which, keep in mind, has a stronger flavor than raw.

Agar

Lastly, agar (actually a seaweed) is widely used in raw desserts because it's a vegan gelatin alternative. To activate the gelatinous texture of agar, it must be heated. The only time I will instruct you to use a stove or boiling water is when agar is used in a recipe.

Although some ingredients are processed and heated, they still provide a lot of nutrition and are essential to creating outstanding raw dessert recipes. Most of us have no idea how ingredients are actually processed, where they come from, their sustainability or the entire journey they took to get from the ground to your home. I encourage you to do your own research, and I feel it's important to have this information so you can decide what you feel comfortable using. Also, most important, use your intuition; our body is the best communicator in letting us know what it likes or doesn't like.

EQUIPMENT AND TOOLS FOR THE RAW KITCHEN

You are not required to use the same tools and brands I do, but I provide recommendations I feel are the best to execute these recipes. The must-have appliances are a high-speed blender, food dehydrator and food processor. A high-speed blender is an essential tool for creating beautiful, smooth frostings and fillings, and is your best investment for creating professional-style raw desserts. Brands I recommend for a high-speed blender are Vitamix, Blendtec® or OmniBlend™.

We do not use an oven in a raw kitchen, so you will need a dehydrator to replace your oven. A food dehydrator removes the water content from food and is temperature controlled, so you're able to keep the temperature below the "raw" threshold of 114° to 118°F (46 to 48°C). Plus, dehydrating is a beautiful way to create garnishes, raw pastries, cakes and cookies. Brands I recommend for a food dehydrator are Excalibur®, Sedona® or BioChef®.

A food processor is also a must-have appliance to make cakes, pies and tart crusts with raw flours. A blender will not create the required consistency because it will quickly release oils from nuts, seeds or coconut, producing more of a nut butter or meal rather than flour.

Another fun appliance to have in your kitchen is a countertop ice-cream maker. I love the Cuisinart® brand as it's fairly priced and great quality. This device is compact and easy to use. In the Creamy Ice Cream without the Dairy chapter (page 119), the recipes turn out best if made with an ice-cream maker, but I also provide instructions on how to make them without one.

Raw cakes should be enjoyed sparingly, which is why I prefer to use small springform cake and tart pans, such as 4- to 4½-inch (10- to 11.5-cm) pans. Plus, an added bonus in creating miniature cakes is that they do not require many ingredients. If you were to make an 8-inch (20-cm) cake, the 4- to 4½-inch (10- to 11.5-cm) cake recipes would need to be doubled. If you already have cake pans and baking tools at home, feel free to use what you have on hand and adjust the recipe up as needed. Note that I also sometimes call for the use of silicone molds, again for desserts served in small portions.

Basic baking tools include piping tips, pastry bags, cookie cutters and a rolling pin. A pastry scraper, offset spatula and cake turntable will make frosting and decorating a cake much easier.

You will be creating your own homemade, plant-based milks and creams, so having a nut milk bag will be handy. Another useful tool is a coconut-opening device. We use young coconut meat instead of dried in frostings, pies and cakes for an ultra creamy experience, but check out the Substitutions List (page 160) for other options.

GETTING FAMILIAR WITH YOUR INGREDIENTS

I highly recommend purchasing most ingredients such as nuts, seeds, grains, coconut oil, dried coconut, dry and liquid sweeteners, nut butters, dried fruit and superfood powders in bulk. Bulk suppliers charge much less than a retailer. For example, the organic bulk supplier I order from charges (at the moment of writing this) $15 for a pound (454 g) of organic raw almonds. If I were to buy the same almonds from the organic grocery store, I would pay double to triple the price. There are many options now available for organic bulk suppliers; a couple of my favorite companies in Canada are Organic Matters and Real Raw Food. In the U.S., popular ones are Organic Essentials and Terrasoul Superfoods.

When using these ingredients and creating recipes at home, the best way to stay organized and prevent errors is by implementing a chef practice called *mise en place*, pronounced "meez ahn plas." This French term means "putting in place" or "everything in place." This technique is used by professional chefs in kitchens, cooking classes, recipe demonstrations and home cooking. Why is this method important?

When you make recipes at home, you've probably experienced running all over the place trying to find equipment, tools and ingredients as you're using them. Not only is this a big time-waster, but it also creates a lot of room for error. Gathering everything beforehand will also save space in your work area, as food containers and packaging take up more space.

Here are some tips for practicing *mise en place*:

- Before putting together any recipe, gather the equipment and tools required and place them near your work area.

- Gather all the ingredients you require for the recipe and place them in your working area. Measure out each ingredient into bowls, making sure to prep and measure each ingredient as written.

Let's dive into some important notes on these nutritious ingredients you will be working with and how to store them for longevity and freshness.

Nuts, Nut Butters & Seeds

We use raw nuts and seeds in the recipes in this book. You will notice almonds are widely used in crusts and cakes because the fat content is just right, they are more neutral in flavor and the most inexpensive nut available.

Raw nuts and seeds only last approximately three months on the shelf at room temperature, but will last much longer in the fridge or freezer, up to one year. I realize not everyone has space in their fridge or freezer to store pounds of ingredients (neither do I), so I have a minifridge on my patio where I keep all my nuts and seeds. I've been using this method for years.

I recommend storing high-fat nuts and seeds, such as walnuts, macadamia nuts, hemp seeds, pumpkin seeds, flaxseeds and hazelnuts, in the fridge or freezer, especially ground flax, since it goes rancid quickly. Dehydrated nuts and seeds, on the other hand, will last much longer on the shelf at room temperature because extra moisture has been removed during dehydrating. Nut butters are shelf-stable, but I prefer to store them in the fridge for optimal freshness, except for coconut butter. Coconut butter keeps well on the shelf at room temperature. Buckwheat is technically a seed and is stable at room temperature in a sealed food-grade container. It will last for several months, but keep an eye on it because buckwheat can attract bugs.

Cacao Products

Cacao butter and cacao paste are solid unless melted; therefore, they are much easier to measure in grams. I recommend measuring these ingredients in grams using a kitchen scale. This also allows for no waste or over- or undermelting the volume required.

Cacao Butter: Cacao butter is a strong binder used widely in chocolate-based recipes to amplify the cacao flavors. It has a higher melting point than coconut oil, so it is much firmer at room temperature or when cooled. To provide a softer result in recipes, using a blend of cacao butter and coconut oil works well.

Cacao Paste: Also called cacao liquor or cacao mass, cacao paste is my first choice in chocolate making because it produces a smoother result than cacao powder. Cacao paste looks solid like cacao butter but is dark brown because it is all parts of the cacao bean pressed into paste.

Cacao products (cacao powder, cacao butter, cacao paste, cacao nibs) have a long shelf life if stored in a cool, dark place with no exposure to light. If your pantry is exposed to sunlight, keep your cacao products in a nonglass container to avoid light exposure.

If the temperature in your house is 93°F (34°C) and above, there is potential for your cacao butter to melt since the melting point of cacao butter is 93 to 100°F (34 to 38°C). In that case, you might want to store it in the fridge. Cacao butter has a long shelf life of two to five years. We dive more into cacao in the Troubleshooting Chocolate section (page 21).

Coconut Products

Coconut Oil: The most popular ingredient used in setting raw desserts is coconut oil because it solidifies in cool temperatures, holding the mixture together. Coconut oil produces a soft, creamy result in cheesecakes, frostings and chocolate. Source only virgin coconut oil (also known as cold-pressed and unrefined) for these recipes; it is the most effective at setting raw desserts. During my kitchen adventures, I have not had a good experience with refined coconut oil in setting desserts as they are not as effective.

Store coconut oil in a sealed food-grade container at room temperature. If you live somewhere warm or it's the summer season, you will notice coconut oil stays liquid because it has a low melting point. Once the weather cools and the temperature in your house cools, it will solidify and require melting before use.

Young Coconuts: Coconuts are one of the most nutritious foods on the planet; classified as a fruit, they are high in minerals, vitamin C and lauric acid, which has antioxidant and antibacterial properties.

Thai young coconuts are widely available from Asian markets, your local organic grocer and now even big chain grocery stores. In some parts of the world, young coconuts are unfortunately difficult to source. They are widely available here in North America and frozen coconut meat is available from a U.S. company called Copra Coconuts. If you cannot source young coconuts, cashews are the best substitution; refer to the Substitutions List (page 160) for more information.

Many excellent coconut-opening tools are available online. Opening coconuts can be intimidating at first, but once you get the hang of it, it's fun! The best way to prep coconut meat is to buy multiple coconuts at once (preferably a case), open them, chop the meat, portion the meat into 1-cup (80-g) measurements and freeze it. That way, when you require coconut meat for a recipe, you already have some in the freezer and you know how much to thaw. Thaw it in the fridge overnight before use.

Young coconuts need to be refrigerated, and once you've removed the coconut flesh, it will keep in the fridge for three days.

Sweeteners

We use a variety of sweeteners in this book and there are a lot of opinions on which sweeteners are labeled healthy. Use sweeteners you feel comfortable with and that feel good for your body.

Liquid Sweeteners: Liquid, dark-amber sweeteners, such as pure maple syrup, agave and coconut nectar, are interchangeable in these recipes. I use light-amber agave in light-colored recipes since it's a vegan alternative to honey. My favorite go-to sweetener is coconut nectar because it's low glycemic and full of minerals. I purchase coconut nectar in bulk from a company in Canada called Real Raw Food. In the U.S. it's available from a company called Copra Coconuts.

Crystallized Sweeteners: In some recipes, for consistency and texture, I prefer to use a dry sweetener, such as coconut sugar or a sugar alcohol called xylitol. Coconut sugar is low glycemic, darker in color and has a caramel aftertaste better paired with darker recipes, such as chocolate. Xylitol is white, so it's great to use in light-colored recipes and fillings, such as the Coconut Frosting (page 148). Xylitol is extremely toxic to dogs, so if you have a pup that gets into your pantry, just in case, using erythritol is a better choice. Also, sugar alcohols are very low on the glycemic index and safe for diabetics.

Store coconut nectar and maple syrup in the fridge. Agave and crystallized sweeteners are stored at room temperature.

Sunflower Lecithin Powder

Outside of culinary use, sunflower lecithin powder is a health supplement; it is made from the sunflower plant and does not contain any additives. It is high in choline, which is excellent for liver health, brain function and digestive health, just to name a few.

It is used in food as an emulsifier, binding fats and liquids together, and commonly replaces eggs in baking. Sunflower lecithin powder is easy to source (it's available on Amazon™); my favorite one to use is the NOW Foods® brand. You can also look for sunflower lecithin powder at your local vitamin store. Try not to skip this ingredient; it makes a big difference in the texture and consistency of the desserts, especially those that contain coconut meat and ice creams, although it is optional in some recipes.

Lecithin should always be stored in the fridge because of its high fat content.

Frozen, Freeze-Dried and Dried Fruits

Frozen Fruits: Compared to fresh fruit, frozen fruit is more accessible and less expensive. It's important to note that frozen fruit, once thawed, produces liquid that may need straining (read those directions carefully). When you're required to use frozen fruit in recipes, measure it first before thawing, then thaw in the refrigerator overnight.

Freeze-Dried Fruits: Once you have broken the seal on any freeze-dried items, store them in the freezer. Freeze-dried food soaks up moisture quickly at room temperature and will go soft, changing the texture. I prefer to use freeze-dried fruit in some recipes over fresh or thawed fruit since freeze-dried fruit produces a creamier result. Fresh or thawed fruit contains water and depending on the recipe, can produce an "icy" texture once cooled.

Dried Fruits: We use unsulfured dried fruits in some recipes, which is the healthier option because there are no added preservatives, such as sulfur dioxide or added sugars. Unsulfured dried fruit such as apricots are darker in color. Dried fruit is more susceptible to attracting bugs, so they are best stored in the fridge. Check dates for worms or black mold when pitting them; the pests are very small and look like darker specks inside the date.

Superfood Powders

If you purchase superfood powders in bulk, they usually come in a temporary storage bag. It's best to remove the contents from the bag and transfer them to a sealed glass Mason jar or food-grade container. Because they are dried, superfood powders will last several months on the shelf at room temperature. Spirulina and chlorella are the only superfood powders I prefer to store in the fridge, to maintain optimal freshness.

Flavor Extracts

I recommend and use extracts made by a U.S. company called Medicine Flower; they are highly concentrated, non-GMO and high quality. This company carries a few lines; I prefer the alcohol-free extracts from the premium line. Some other comparable extract brands available are Nature's Flavors, available in the U.S., and, in the United Kingdom, where they are called essences, Foodie Flavours™. These extracts are optional and only a recommendation; feel free to use the extracts you already have in your pantry. Five drops of vanilla Medicine Flower brand equals 1 teaspoon of vanilla extract from other brands.

PREP NOTES

I'm a big believer in using ingredients that have been sprouted, activated and made from scratch! Using less processed ingredients elevates the nutritional value of your recipes. Take the time to prep these ingredients ahead of time; it will simplify and ease the process of creating these recipes and create efficiency in the kitchen.

Powdered Pantry Staples

Powdered Psyllium: Psyllium is a fiber that acts as a binder. It absorbs moisture quickly and thickens batters; a little goes a long way. We use powdered psyllium in recipes that are typically "doughier," such as the Mocha Donuts with Espresso Glaze (page 92) and the Three-Layer Tiramisu Cake (page 81). Psyllium is generally sold in husk form; if not broken down into a powder in recipes, it produces a grainy texture. I prefer to powder it first to break it down, so it will incorporate easier. When a recipe calls for powdered psyllium, measure it after it's powdered.

1 cup (80 g) psyllium husk

In a dry high-speed blender or spice grinder, blend the psyllium husk until it forms a powder. Transfer to a small Mason jar or food-grade container and store it at room temperature until ready to use.

Powdered Coconut Sugar: Coconut sugar is one of my favorite sweeteners to use in raw desserts; it's low glycemic, high in minerals and generally one of the least expensive sweeteners. It's darker in color, so it pairs well in darker-colored recipes, including chocolate. Coconut sugar comes in crystal form, so it's grainy in texture if not broken down properly. You will notice some recipes do not require powdered coconut sugar because you want added texture in that recipe. Watch for the difference in how we use coconut sugar.

2 cups (320 g) coconut sugar

In a dry high-speed blender or spice grinder, blend the coconut sugar until it forms a powder. If using a spice grinder, you will need to blend in small batches. Transfer to a Mason jar or food-grade container and store it at room temperature until ready to use.

Powdered Xylitol: Xylitol is a sugar alcohol that has only a 7 rating on the glycemic index, making it diabetic friendly. I prefer to use light-colored sweeteners, such as sugar alcohols, in light-colored desserts and frostings. Xylitol is very toxic for dogs, so if you're worried about your pups getting into your pantry, I would suggest using erythritol instead.

2 cups (390 g) xylitol

In a dry high-speed blender or spice grinder, blend the xylitol until it forms a powder. If using a spice grinder, you will need to blend in small batches. Transfer to a Mason jar or food-grade container and store it at room temperature until ready to use.

Ground Golden Flax: Flaxseeds are a staple in raw recipes and act as a "glue" to bind ingredients together because they absorb water and create a gelatinous mixture. Flax is high in omega-3s and easily prone to oxidation, so it's important to grind your own flax instead of purchasing flax meal. I prefer to use only golden flax instead of brown flax as it's lighter in color and will not affect the color of the recipes. Flax can be bitter in flavor, but we are not using a large amount that will overpower the taste of these recipes.

2 cups (336 g) golden flaxseeds

In a dry high-speed blender or spice grinder, blend the flaxseeds until they become flax meal. If using a spice grinder, you will need to blend in small batches. Transfer to a Mason jar and store it in the freezer for optimal freshness. Flax goes rancid quickly, so it's best to store it in the fridge or freezer.

Processing Crusts and Batters

Crusts and batters for cookies and raw pastries are best processed in a food processor, not a blender. This is because blending such ingredients as nuts, seeds or coconut will cause the oils to release quickly and will start turning into butters. We don't want our crusts too oily, so using a food processor is more effective. We usually create a flour base first, then add the wet ingredients to bind the mixture together. Using this method, you will process the mixture successfully.

It's best to place your crusts aside at room temperature while you make fillings for recipes, rather than chilling them in the fridge or freezer. This is because fillings usually contain a setting agent, such as coconut oil or cacao butter, so the filling will start to set quickly if added to a cold crust, not allowing you enough time to even out the filling and remove any air bubbles.

If a crust is too wet or too oily, add ½ teaspoon of coconut flour or more (if required) to the mixture in the food processor and process until combined. Coconut flour absorbs moisture quickly and will help dry out the mixture.

Blending

The type of blender you are using will determine the length of time required to blend. If using a high-speed blender, such as a Vitamix, OmniBlend or Blendtec, always start on low speed and increase to medium or high speed. If you blend too long on high speed, the ingredients will start to warm due to friction from the blades.

When blending chocolate recipes, blend on low to medium speed to avoid heating the chocolate mixture; otherwise, it will start to thicken too fast and become difficult to incorporate. Learn more about chocolate in the Troubleshooting Chocolate section on page 21.

Melting/Liquefying

How you melt and liquefy ingredients will affect them significantly. There are two main melting methods that I prefer to use:

The Double Boiler Method: A double boiler consists of placing the ingredient(s) to be melted in the top section of a double boiler or in a heatproof bowl that is set atop a pot. The lower pot should be filled partway with water (not touching the top pot or bowl) that is then heated on a stovetop.

- **Virgin Coconut Oil:** Only use low to medium heat, and as soon as the coconut oil starts to melt, remove the pot from the heat, stirring the coconut oil until it's melted. Virgin (unrefined) coconut oil will not set desserts effectively if overheated. If you are in a pinch, using a microwave is not the healthiest method, but it does work. Just make sure to microwave coconut oil for no more than 45 seconds.

- **Coconut Butter:** As this has a high melting point and it is not required to be fully liquefied before used in recipes, I prefer the term "softened" coconut butter. Soften the coconut butter using the double boiler method until it's soft enough to measure and then incorporate in your recipe.

The Bowl Over Bowl Method: I prefer to use this method because there is much less room for error than using the stove, since the stove produces more heat. Fill a stainless-steel bowl with boiling water from a kettle, then place the ingredients to be melted in a second stainless-steel bowl (bigger than the bowl of water, so it doesn't rest on the water) and rest that bowl on top of the smaller bowl.

- **Cacao Butter and Cacao Paste:** Chop cacao butter and cacao paste into small pieces before melting for a quicker melting process. Cacao is the most fragile ingredient of them all (believe it or not)! Cacao burns very easily; if you can avoid using a microwave, please do! I prefer to use this method to melt cacao butter and cacao paste to prevent burning them on the stove. Cacao paste takes a little more time to melt; it melts best when the cacao butter is on the bottom of the upper bowl first, then the cacao paste is added to it. Note that, in some recipes, cacao butter or cacao paste must be measured precisely in grams prior to melting; however, in other recipes, it is melted first and then measured in U.S. spoons/cups or grams.

- **Enrobing Dark Chocolate:** When you have leftover Enrobing Dark Chocolate (page 156), you will need to melt it down again before use. Since liquid sweetener is used in the recipe, it has the potential to burn. Cacao requires a lot of patience, so please be patient when melting cacao and use low heat—you will be happy you did. Make sure to refer to my tips on Troubleshooting Chocolate on the next page.

While making the recipes, I prefer to add liquefied ingredients last because some of the ingredients we use are cool in temperature, and these ingredients set in cool environments. If you were to add them with the ingredients before you start blending or processing, the mixture would be more difficult to blend and thicken.

Activating Nuts and Seeds

Most raw nuts and seeds contain phytic acid, which is necessary to protect them in the early stages of growth. Although this acid is not toxic to humans, it inhibits the absorption of nutrients. Soaking the raw nuts and seeds for the recommended time ensures the phytic acid is neutralized and will aid in digestion.

To activate nuts and seeds, soak them in a glass jar or bowl. Follow the soaking chart for soaking times of different varieties. Use filtered water, if possible; otherwise, use cold tap water. Add enough water so they are completely submerged, then cover the bowl or jar with a clean tea towel or lid to prevent contamination. Once they are done soaking, strain, rinse well and use in recipes as required. If a recipe calls for dehydrated nuts, dehydrate them on a lined dehydrator tray at 115°F (46°C) for 12 to 24 hours, or until fully dried. Almonds require 24 hours of drying time.

Refer to this soaking chart for the recommended soaking times. Some nuts and/or seeds do not require soaking because they contain very low phytic acid content, but it's a good habit to rinse them to remove dust and debris or soak them to soften for blending.

Soaking Time Chart

Nuts/Seeds	Soaking Time
Almonds	8 to 12 hours
Brazil nuts	No soaking required; rinse or soak to soften for blending
Cashews	2 hours
Hazelnuts	No soaking required; rinse or soak to soften for blending
Hemp seeds	No soaking or rinsing required
Macadamia nuts	No soaking required; rinse or soak to soften for blending
Pecans	4 to 6 hours
Pistachios	No soaking required; rinse or soak to soften for blending
Pumpkin seeds	8 hours
Sunflower seeds	2 hours
Walnuts	4 hours

Troubleshooting Chocolate

Chocolate is one of the more challenging ingredients to work with, and I bet every pastry chef would agree. Cocoa or cacao butter is made up of molecules formed in six different ways (crystal formations), depending on the temperature of the cocoa butter. As cocoa butter heats and cools, different crystal formations occur, causing chocolate's different states, from melted to solid. There is much to learn about chocolate, and I won't go into too much detail, but I include the essential information you require to successfully execute the recipes in this book.

Some Tips on Getting Started

- Make sure your equipment is dry.

- There should be no humidifiers operating in your house nor steam emitting from a stovetop.

- There should be no water close to your chocolate-making area.

- If your tools are wet, dry them in a dehydrator.

Seized Chocolate

- "Seizing" refers to when your chocolate thickens up and is no longer liquefied. When chocolate is seized, it looks grainy and thick like fudge.

- This happens if chocolate overheats, liquid is introduced or cold ingredients have been introduced, since chocolate sets in a cold environment.

- How do you fix this if it happens? Depending on the state of the chocolate, add a little room-temperature liquid (water or nut milk) and whisk it until the batch has thinned out again. If it has thickened because it's cooled, warm it up in a double boiler (see page 19) or by using a hair dryer, heating the bowl from underneath.

- Seizing can also be done on purpose to cause chocolate to thicken, creating a fudgelike consistency or chocolate sauce! Warm and cold water can be used to produce this—the important thing is that a change in temperature takes place. We use warm water to create a fudge consistency in recipes such as Orange Hazelnut Fudge (page 37) and Dark Chocolate Ganache (page 153), and room-temperature water in the Chocolate Sauce (page 154).

Enrobing

- The Enrobing Dark Chocolate recipe (page 156) is used to coat a product with chocolate.

- Some tips while working with enrobing chocolate are to use a small bowl so you have more control over the volume and to keep a hair dryer close by to heat the Enrobing Dark Chocolate (page 156) when it starts setting during the enrobing process.

Chocolate requires practice and patience; don't be afraid to get messy, make mistakes and experiment. Once you become more comfortable working with chocolate, it's a lot of fun and very satisfying!

THE BUILDING-BLOCK RECIPES

I'm a big believer in using fewer store-bought, processed ingredients and making your own homemade versions. Not only are the homemade versions more nutritious, they are generally less expensive. Save money and boost your health at the same time—a win-win! For the recipes in this book, you will use homemade nut milks and creams, as well as coconut milks and creams. Store-bought vegan milks are laced with unnecessary ingredients and mostly contain water and thickeners. If you've never tried homemade nut milks before, they are a game-changer!

When making your own homemade plant milks, the standard ratio is one part nuts, seeds or coconut to four parts water (preferably filtered). The standard ratio for creating cream is one to two parts. You can also play around with the ratios and adjust the consistency to your liking. Just think of the different possibilities you can make by using a variety of nuts and seeds!

You will also make activated, living oat flour for use in raw pastries, crusts, cakes and tarts. Activated Oat Flour (page 28) has the same texture as wheat flour; you will love working with it. Also included is a probiotic-rich, gut-friendly cheesecake base we use in cultured cheesecakes and a recipe for smooth, homemade Coconut Butter (page 31).

ALMOND MILK

Yield: 4 cups (960 ml)

Probably the most popular vegan milk, the homemade version is genuinely different than store-bought. It's creamier and much tastier without all the added ingredients. We use almond milk in multiple recipes throughout the book. Remember to reserve the pulp to use in other recipes.

In a blender, blend the almonds and water together for 30 seconds to 1 minute. Place a nut milk bag in a bowl (it's easiest to use one with a spout), pour the mixture into the nut milk bag and squeeze the nut milk bag to release the milk into the bowl. Transfer the milk to a Mason jar. Store in the fridge for up to 3 days.

*See image on page 22.

1 cup (145 g) raw almonds, soaked for 8 hours and rinsed

4 cups (960 ml) water

PRO TIP: Save the almond pulp; we use this in recipes throughout the book and it is a great low-waste ingredient! Transfer the almond pulp to a food-grade container and store in the fridge for 3 days or in the freezer for up to 1 month. If frozen, thaw in the fridge for 8 hours before use.

BRAZIL NUT MILK

Brazil nut milk is one of my favorite plant milks because of its ultra creamy consistency. I love to use this in the base of ice creams.

Yield: 2 cups (480 ml)

In a blender, blend the Brazil nuts and water together for 30 seconds to 1 minute. Place a nut milk bag in a bowl (it's easiest to use one with a spout), pour the mixture into the nut milk bag and squeeze the nut milk bag to release the milk into the bowl. Transfer the milk to a Mason jar. Store in the fridge for up to 3 days.

½ cup (67 g) raw Brazil nuts, rinsed
2 cups (480 ml) water

HAZELNUT MILK

We use hazelnut milk in the Chocolate Hazelnut Praline Tarts (page 105) to complement the decadence of that recipe. This milk is rich on its own and full of flavor.

Yield: 2½ cups (600 ml)

In a blender, blend the hazelnuts and water together for 30 seconds to 1 minute. Place a nut milk bag in a bowl (it's easiest to use one with a spout), pour the mixture into the nut milk bag and squeeze the nut milk bag to release the milk into the bowl. Transfer the milk to a Mason jar. Store in the fridge for up to 3 days.

½ cup (67 g) raw hazelnuts, rinsed
2 cups (480 ml) water

PISTACHIO MILK

Yield: 1½ cups (360 ml)

We use pistachio milk to create the Strawberry Rose Pistachio Cream Slice (page 140). We use less water in this recipe to achieve a thicker consistency.

In a blender, blend the pistachios and water together for 30 seconds to 1 minute. Place a nut milk bag in a bowl (it's easiest to use one with a spout), pour the mixture into the nut milk bag and squeeze the nut milk bag to release the milk into the bowl. Transfer the milk to a Mason jar. Store in the fridge for up to 3 days.

½ cup (64 g) raw pistachios, rinsed

1½ cups (360 ml) water

PECAN MILK

Yield: 2 cups (480 ml)

Pecan milk is nuttier in flavor, rich and creamy. We use it in the Pecan Pie with Rosemary and Orange (page 107) filling to bring out the decadence of that recipe.

In a blender, blend the pecans and water together for 30 seconds to 1 minute. Place a nut milk bag in a bowl (it's easiest to use one with a spout), pour the mixture into the nut milk bag and squeeze the nut milk bag to release the milk into the bowl. Transfer the milk to a Mason jar. Store in the fridge for up to 3 days.

½ cup (50 g) pecans, soaked for 4 hours and rinsed

2 cups (480 ml) water

COCONUT MILK

Making your own coconut milk from dried coconut is really easy. We use it in some of the recipes, such as the Milk Chocolate Cherry Cinnamon Truffles (page 40) and Coconut Frosting (page 148).

Yield: 4 cups (960 ml)

In a blender, blend the shredded coconut and water together for 30 seconds to 1 minute. Place a nut milk bag in a bowl (it's easiest to use one with a spout), pour the mixture into the nut milk bag and squeeze the nut milk bag to release the milk into the bowl. Transfer the milk to a Mason jar. Store in the fridge for up to 3 days.

1 cup (85 g) fine- or medium-shred unsweetened dried coconut

4 cups (960 ml) water

PRO TIP: Save the coconut pulp; we use this in recipes throughout the book and it is a great low-waste ingredient! Transfer the coconut pulp to a container and store in the fridge for 3 days or in the freezer for up to 1 month. If frozen, thaw in the fridge for 8 hours before use.

COCONUT CREAM

Instead of using canned coconut cream, we make our own from scratch! Make sure to reserve the coconut pulp, as we use it in the Lemon Poppy Seed Coconut Shortbread Cookies (page 86).

Yield: 2 cups (480 ml)

In a blender, blend the shredded coconut and water together for 30 seconds to 1 minute. Place a nut milk bag in a bowl (it's easiest to use one with a spout), pour the mixture into the nut milk bag and squeeze the nut milk bag to release the cream into the bowl. Transfer the cream to a Mason jar. Store in the fridge for up to 3 days.

1 cup (85 g) fine- or medium-shred unsweetened dried coconut

2 cups (480 ml) water

PRO TIP: Save the coconut pulp; we use this in recipes throughout the book and it is a great low-waste ingredient! Transfer the coconut pulp to a container and store in the fridge for 3 days or in the freezer for up to 1 month. If frozen, thaw in the fridge for 8 hours before use.

ACTIVATED OAT FLOUR

Yield: 3¾ cups (488 g)

Raw, activated oat flour is a fun ingredient because it's nutritious, homemade, living and an excellent alternative to wheat flour. You will love the texture of it. This book uses activated oat flour in raw pastries, cookies and cake bases, such as the Mocha Donuts with Espresso Glaze (page 92), Matcha Raspberry Linzer Cookies (page 89) and the Mocha Crisp Cheesecake (page 64). Make sure to use oat groats as they have not been processed or heat-treated. If you have a gluten allergy, purchase gluten-free oat groats. If you are unable to source oat groats, check out the Substitutions List (page 160) for other options.

In a bowl, soak the oat groats with enough water to cover for 6 to 8 hours, then strain and rinse well. Spread the groats on a lined dehydrator tray and dehydrate at 115°F (46°C) for 12 to 20 hours, or until dried. Ensure your high-speed blender jug is fully dry, then blend the dehydrated oat groats in two separate batches until a flour is formed.

Sift the oat flour through a fine-mesh strainer or sieve over a dry bowl to remove any leftover unblended, hard granules. If the flour still looks grainy, repeat the blending and sifting process. Store the oat flour in the freezer for optimal freshness.

5 cups raw oat groats (900 g)

Water

SPROUTED AND DEHYDRATED BUCKWHEAT

Despite its name, buckwheat is a gluten-free seed and a great source of protein and fiber. We use sprouted and dehydrated buckwheat in many recipes throughout the cookbook. It's a versatile ingredient, excellent in granolas and in raw pastry, cake and chocolate bar bases. After dehydration, it's very crunchy, making it a wonderful element to add texture to your desserts. Make sure to use raw buckwheat groats; if they are roasted, they will not sprout (the roasted type is usually called kasha).

Yield: 2 cups (260 g)

In a bowl, soak the buckwheat with enough water to cover for 20 minutes, then rinse well and strain. Leave the buckwheat in the strainer and place it over a bowl to catch the water. Place a clean tea towel over the top of the strainer and set aside at room temperature for 24 to 36 hours to sprout, rinsing two or three times a day. The sprouting process is complete when the tail is the same size as the width of your pinkie finger.

Rinse well one more time, strain and spread on a lined dehydrator tray. Dehydrate at 115°F (46°C) for 8 to 12 hours, or until dried. Store at room temperature until ready to use.

2 cups (260 g) raw buckwheat groats
Water

CULTURED CASHEW FILLING

Culture your own cashew filling at home to make cheesecakes. Culturing is a fermentation process whereby a microbial starter, such as probiotics, is used. Culturing the cashews makes the cakes easier to digest and adds a healthy dose of probiotics to your gut. It is wonderful to use in raw cheesecakes to add to that tangy, "cheesy" flavor. Using an excellent high-speed blender for this recipe is critical as the mixture is quite thick.

Yield: About 2 cups (475 ml)

Before fermenting at home, sterilize all equipment you're using for this recipe by running them through the dishwasher on the sanitize cycle or soaking them in equal parts hot water and white vinegar in your sink and rinsing them well. Open the two probiotics capsules and pour their contents into a high-speed blender. Add the soaked cashews and filtered water, and blend until incorporated. The mixture does not need to be entirely smooth as it will be combined again in the recipes to achieve a smooth texture.

Transfer the mixture to a glass bowl and cover the bowl with cling film or parchment paper and an elastic to seal it. Cover the bowl with an additional tea towel to ensure it's not exposed to light. UV light destroys good bacteria during the fermentation process. Place the bowl in a warm area for 12 to 24 hours. If you do not have a warm spot in your house, place it in a microwave with its door closed. A microwave is usually much warmer than the outside ambient temperature.

The longer you leave the mixture to culture, the tangier it will taste. Feel free to taste it every 12 hours until it is at your desired taste. If the mixture has formed a crust on top, that is fine—it will be blended and incorporated. If you're not ready to make the dessert that calls for this filling, but the cashews are tangy enough, place it in the fridge to stop the fermentation.

2 capsules dairy-free probiotics (15 billion strains or more)

2 cups (280 g) raw cashews, soaked for 2 hours and rinsed

¼ cup (60 ml) filtered water

PRO TIP: One full batch is enough for recipes with two 4½-inch (11.5-cm) cakes.

COCONUT BUTTER

Yield: 1½ cups (360 g)

Homemade coconut butter is cost-effective and simple to make. The key to blending the dried coconut is to add melted coconut oil. Coconut butter is a beautiful setting agent and addition to coconut fillings. If you're using a wide-based Vitamix jug, you will need to double the recipe for the batch to blend smoothly.

To a high-speed blender, add 2 cups (130 g) of the large flake or (170 g) of the shredded coconut, followed by 2 tablespoons (30 ml) of the melted coconut oil. Blend on low to medium speed until the mixture has broken down. You will require a tamper for this.

Add 1 more cup (65 g) of the large flake or (85 g) of the shredded coconut and blend until the mixture breaks down even more. Add the last cup of coconut and blend until smooth. Only if required and the mixture is having difficulty blending, add the last tablespoon (15 ml) of melted coconut oil.

Like nut butter, coconut butter keeps for months at room temperature in a glass container. Soften before adding to recipes by using the double boiler method (see page 19).

PRO TIP: Coconut butter will not fully melt but will soften enough to blend and process into recipes.

4 cups (260 g) large flake or 4 cups (320 g) medium-shred unsweetened dried coconut, divided

2 to 3 tbsp (30-45 ml) melted virgin coconut oil, as needed

AGAR PASTE

Yield: 1 cup (240 ml)

Agar, also known as agar-agar or kanten, is a flavorless gelling agent derived from red seaweed, used as a vegan gelatin alternative. Commonly used in desserts to replace fat content, it acts as a setting agent and binder. Agar requires heat to be activated, so it is not considered raw.

In a teakettle or pot, bring the water to a boil on a stovetop. In a blender, blend the agar powder with the hot water for 30 seconds to combine. Be careful while blending; you are working with boiling water that is very hot. Transfer the agar mixture to a small Mason jar and let it sit at room temperature to cool. Use immediately or keep in the fridge until ready to use. Once cooled, the agar mixture will become a paste and resemble prepared gelatin. Agar paste will keep in the refrigerator for up to 1 week.

1 cup (240 ml) water

1 tbsp (7 g) agar powder

HEAVENLY CHOCOLATE AND TRUFFLES

The chocolate chapter! Chocolate is the love of my life; I cannot go a day without it. Whether you're into dark chocolate, white chocolate or fruity chocolate, there is a recipe in this chapter for everyone. Fudge, truffles and chocolate bars are included, with two flavors of each. You will love the Buckwheat Crunch Chocolate Bars with Apricot Jam (page 44) if you love pairing a crunchy texture and chocolate together. If you're a fan of mint and chocolate, you have to try the White Chocolate Peppermint Fudge (page 34). The Milk Chocolate Cherry Cinnamon Truffles (page 40) are so creamy and delicious, I bet you won't be able to eat just one.

I highly recommend reviewing The Foundations of Creating Raw Desserts chapter (page 11) before getting started on this chapter or working with chocolate in general. Chocolate can be one of the most challenging ingredients to work with, making it that much more rewarding. It's also super fun and, of course, delicious!

WHITE CHOCOLATE PEPPERMINT FUDGE

These are reminiscent of a Canadian treat called an After Eight®, except better. The fudge is creamy with the added minted candied cacao nibs for some crunch and is a great recipe to make during the holidays. I love using a small brownie silicone mold for fudge, but feel free to use any silicone mold you already have at home. Check out the Substitutions List (page 160) for other options for the peppermint essential oil and xylitol.

Yield: 24 pieces

MINTED CANDIED CACAO NIBS

In a stainless-steel or heatproof glass bowl, combine the chopped cacao butter and cacao paste and melt them together very carefully, using the double boiler method (page 19), making sure not to burn the chocolate. While the bowl is still on the heat, add the coconut nectar, peppermint essential oil and vanilla and stir until incorporated.

Remove the bowl from the heat and let the chocolate sit at room temperature for 15 minutes to cool, speeding up the cooling process by transferring the melted chocolate to a fresh, unheated bowl. If you add the cacao nibs too early, they will melt. Add the cacao nibs and mix well until combined.

Transfer the chocolate to a lined shallow container or baking sheet and let it set in the fridge or freezer for 1 hour. Transfer the chocolate to a food processor and process until a crumble is formed. Store it in the refrigerator until ready to use.

WHITE CHOCOLATE PEPPERMINT FUDGE

In a high-speed blender, blend together the cashews, melted cacao butter, xylitol, agave, melted coconut oil, lucuma powder, peppermint essential oil, vanilla and salt until smooth. The mixture will be thick and look grainy, but it will emulsify and smooth out once you add the water. Add the warm water and blend on low speed until combined.

To the fudge mixture in the blender, add the minted candied cacao nibs, but set a handful aside to use for assembling the fudge later on. Stir them in by hand. Place a small brownie silicone mold with 1⅜-inch (3.5-cm) cavities on a cutting board or tray and fill the mold with the entire fudge mixture. Chill the fudge in the freezer overnight or for a minimum of 8 hours, until firm.

(continued)

Minted Candied Cacao Nibs

30 g chopped cacao butter

90 g chopped cacao paste

2 tbsp (30 ml) coconut nectar

5 drops food-grade peppermint essential oil

4 drops vanilla extract, Medicine Flower brand preferred

⅓ cup (40 g) cacao nibs

White Chocolate Peppermint Fudge

¾ cup (105 g) raw cashews, soaked for 2 hours and rinsed

½ cup (100 g) chopped and melted cacao butter

¼ cup (48 g) xylitol

¼ cup (85 g) light-amber agave

¼ cup (60 ml) melted virgin coconut oil

2 tbsp (15 g) lucuma powder

6 drops food-grade peppermint essential oil

4 drops vanilla extract, Medicine Flower brand preferred

Pinch of Himalayan salt

¼ cup (60 ml) warm water

½ cup (62.5 g) Minted Candied Cacao Nibs

WHITE CHOCOLATE
PEPPERMINT FUDGE (continued)

ASSEMBLY

Make or melt the enrobing dark chocolate and transfer to a small bowl. Remove the silicone mold from the freezer and remove each piece of fudge from the mold. Line a cutting board or tray with parchment paper to create an area onto which to put the enrobed fudge.

Using a chocolate dipping fork or regular dinner fork, dip a piece of fudge into the melted chocolate for a few seconds and remove, keeping the fudge on the fork to let the excess chocolate drip off. Transfer the enrobed fudge to your lined surface and repeat the process until each piece of fudge is enrobed.

Fill a piping bag with white chocolate sauce, cut the tip to create a small hole and drizzle each piece of fudge. Garnish with some extra minted candied cacao nibs and/or fresh mint. Enjoy immediately or chill the fudge in the fridge for 30 minutes to set. Store in the refrigerator for 1 week or in the freezer for up to 1 month. Note that if stored in the freezer, the chocolate will create condensation when thawing.

Assembly

1 batch Enrobing Dark Chocolate (page 156)

1 batch White Chocolate Sauce (page 158)

Minted Candied Cacao Nibs

Fresh mint leaves

ORANGE HAZELNUT FUDGE

Orange and hazelnut are a winning combination, especially around the holidays. This recipe is straightforward yet tasty, loaded with texture from the hazelnuts and flavor from the orange essential oil. Check out the Substitutions List (page 160) for other options for the orange essential oil. The contrast of the white chocolate orange drizzle on the dark chocolate fudge is stunning!

Yield: 24 pieces

CARAMELIZED HAZELNUTS

In a food processor, process the hazelnuts, coconut sugar, mesquite powder, coconut nectar, vanilla and salt to reach a large-crumble consistency. Spread the mixture on a lined dehydrator tray and dehydrate at 115°F (46°C) for 18 to 24 hours. The hazelnuts will still be sticky, but they will firm up like a praline once cooled.

Transfer the caramelized hazelnuts to an open container and chill in the freezer for 30 minutes to crisp and firm up. Once cooled, transfer them to a food processor and process them again to break them up if they are stuck together. These will be added to the fudge for extra flavor and texture. You will use ½ cup (68 g) of the caramelized hazelnuts in this recipe and have some left over. They make a wonderful snack; add them to granola, oatmeal and ice cream.

ORANGE CHOCOLATE FUDGE

In a high-speed blender, blend together the cacao powder, coconut sugar, melted cacao butter, coconut nectar, melted coconut oil, hazelnut butter, orange zest, orange essential oil and vanilla until smooth. Add the warm water and blend on low speed until combined. For more information on why we use warm water to create fudge, refer to the Troubleshooting Chocolate section (page 21).

To the fudge mixture in the blender, add the caramelized hazelnuts and stir in by hand. Place a small brownie silicone mold with 1⅜-inch (3.5-cm) cavities on a cutting board or tray and fill the mold with the entire fudge mixture. Chill the fudge in the freezer overnight or for a minimum of 8 hours, until firm.

(continued)

Caramelized Hazelnuts

1 cup (135 g) raw hazelnuts, soaked for 1 hour and rinsed

¼ cup (40 g) coconut sugar

1 tbsp (8 g) mesquite powder

2 tbsp (30 ml) coconut nectar

8 drops vanilla extract, Medicine Flower brand preferred

⅛ tsp Himalayan salt

Orange Chocolate Fudge

½ cup (48 g) cacao powder

½ cup (80 g) coconut sugar

½ cup (100 g) chopped and melted cacao butter

¼ cup (60 ml) coconut nectar

¼ cup (60 ml) melted virgin coconut oil

¼ cup (64 g) hazelnut butter

2 tsp (4 g) orange zest

6 drops food-grade orange essential oil

4 drops vanilla extract, Medicine Flower brand preferred

¼ cup (60 ml) warm water

½ cup (68 g) Caramelized Hazelnuts

ORANGE HAZELNUT FUDGE
(continued)

WHITE CHOCOLATE ORANGE DRIZZLE

In a high-speed blender, blend together the cashews, water, melted cacao butter, agave, orange essential oil, vanilla and turmeric until smooth. Set aside while you enrobe the fudge.

ASSEMBLY

Make or melt the enrobing dark chocolate and transfer the melted chocolate to a small bowl. Remove the silicone mold from the freezer and remove each piece of fudge from the mold. Line a cutting board or tray with parchment paper.

Using a chocolate dipping fork or regular dinner fork, dip each piece of fudge, right side up, into the melted chocolate for a few seconds. Remove the fudge from the chocolate and allow the excess chocolate to drip off. Transfer the enrobed chocolate fudge to the lined surface and repeat the process until each piece of fudge is enrobed.

Transfer the white chocolate orange drizzle to a piping bag and cut the tip to create a small hole. Drizzle each piece of fudge with the white chocolate orange drizzle. Enjoy immediately or chill the fudge in the fridge for 30 minutes to set. Store in the refrigerator for 1 week or the freezer for up to 1 month. Note that if stored in the freezer, the chocolate will create condensation when thawing.

White Chocolate Orange Drizzle

¾ cup (105 g) raw cashews, soaked for 2 hours and rinsed

¼ cup + 2 tbsp (90 ml) water

40 g chopped cacao butter, melted

2 tbsp (43 ml) light-amber agave

3 drops food-grade orange essential oil

2 drops vanilla extract, Medicine Flower brand preferred

¼ tsp ground turmeric

Assembly

1 batch Enrobing Dark Chocolate (page 156)

MILK CHOCOLATE CHERRY CINNAMON TRUFFLES

These raw vegan chocolate truffles are made without dates and produce a creamy texture with an explosion of flavor. To elevate these decadent chocolate truffles, chopped dried tart cherries, cinnamon and lemon zest are added since acidity balances chocolate well. Finished with a chocolate dip for a professional look, these truffles are stunning but super simple to make. Replace the Almond Milk (page 24) with Coconut Milk (page 27) for a nut-free version. Check out the Substitutions List (page 160) for other options for the black cherry extract.

Yield: 30 truffles

CHERRY TRUFFLE FILLING

In a blender, blend together the almond milk, cacao powder, coconut nectar, lemon zest, cinnamon, salt, vanilla and black cherry extract until smooth. Add the melted coconut oil, melted cacao butter and cacao paste, and blend again until combined. Add the chopped tart cherries and manually stir them into the mixture with a spatula.

Transfer the chocolate truffle mixture to a shallow container; it is essential that it is shallow since the dried cherries will sink to the bottom, and you want them to be evenly distributed throughout the filling. Chill the mixture in the fridge for a minimum of 8 hours or overnight, until firm.

Remove the filling from the fridge. Using the large end of a melon baller or a small spoon, scoop out about 1½ teaspoons (8 g) of the filling and roll it into a ball, using your hands. I prefer to wear disposable gloves for this process, as the heat from your hands will melt the filling, making them difficult to roll. Transfer the rolled truffles to a container lined with parchment paper. Repeat this process for the entire batch of filling, then chill the truffles in the freezer for 4 to 6 hours to firm up and cool before enrobing.

TRUFFLE COATING

Make or melt the enrobing dark chocolate and transfer it to a small bowl. Enrobe each truffle by dipping it into the chocolate for a few seconds, removing the truffle with a fork, scraping the excess chocolate drip on the side of the bowl and transferring the enrobed truffle to a tray lined with parchment paper. Repeat this process until all the truffles are enrobed.

Transfer the remaining enrobing dark chocolate to a piping bag, cut off the tip to create a small hole and drizzle the chocolate on top of all the truffles. By the time you're done, they should be set at room temperature and ready to eat. If not, place them in the fridge for 10 minutes to set. If not consumed immediately, store the truffles in the fridge for 1 week or in the freezer for 1 month. Note that if stored in the freezer, the chocolate will create condensation when thawing.

Cherry Truffle Filling

⅓ cup (80 ml) Almond Milk (page 24)

½ cup (48 g) cacao powder

½ cup (120 ml) coconut nectar

1½ tsp (3 g) lemon zest

1 tsp ground cinnamon

⅛ tsp Himalayan salt

6 drops vanilla extract, Medicine Flower brand preferred

6 drops black cherry extract, Medicine Flower brand preferred

2 tbsp (30 ml) melted virgin coconut oil

¼ cup (50 g) chopped and melted cacao butter

¼ cup (50 g) chopped and melted cacao paste

3 tbsp (23 g) chopped dried tart cherries

Truffle Coating

1 batch Enrobing Dark Chocolate (page 156)

LAVENDER BERRY WHITE CHOCOLATE TRUFFLES

These creamy truffles possess a few layers of flavors: blueberry, lavender and vanilla. This is a fun recipe to do with your family; create an assembly line and have fun with the two different truffle coatings! If you're not a fan of floral flavors, feel free to omit the lavender essential oil. We use different coatings for these truffles, so make sure to have some prepared before assembling these.

Yield: 28 truffles

WHITE CHOCOLATE TRUFFLE FILLING

In a high-speed blender, blend the cashews, blueberries, coconut nectar, lemon juice, lavender essential oil and vanilla together until smooth. Add the melted cacao butter and blend again until combined. Transfer the mixture to a container and chill in the fridge for a minimum of 6 hours or overnight, until firm.

Remove the truffle filling from the fridge and, using the large end of a melon baller or a small spoon, scoop about 1½ teaspoons (8 g) of filling, rolling it in a ball shape using your hands. I prefer to wear disposable gloves for this process, as the heat from your hands will melt the filling, making them difficult to roll. Transfer the rolled truffles to a container lined with parchment paper. Repeat this process for the entire batch of filling and chill the truffles in the freezer for 2 hours, to firm up and cool before enrobing.

TRUFFLE COATINGS

Make or melt the enrobing dark chocolate and transfer it to a small bowl. You should already have prepared the candied cacao nibs; place those in their own bowl. Mix the shredded coconut and freeze-dried berry powder in a separate small bowl and line a tray with parchment paper. You should have one bowl of enrobing chocolate and two bowls with different coatings.

ASSEMBLY

Enrobe each truffle by dipping it into the chocolate for a few seconds and removing the truffle with a fork, scraping the excess chocolate drip on the side of the bowl. Working quickly (as the chocolate will start to set), place the enrobed truffle in either the bowl of berry-coconut mixture or in the bowl of candied cacao nibs and coat the truffle, using your hands. Repeat this process, alternating the coatings, and transfer the truffle to a parchment paper–lined tray or cutting board.

Repeat this process until all truffles are enrobed and coated. By the time you're done, they should be set at room temperature and ready to eat. If not, chill them in the fridge for 10 minutes to set. Serve immediately or store in the fridge for 1 week or in the freezer for 1 month. Note that if stored in the freezer, the chocolate will create condensation when thawing.

White Chocolate Truffle Filling

1 cup (140 g) raw cashews, soaked for 2 hours and rinsed

½ cup (65 g) frozen blueberries, thawed (measured before thawing)

¼ cup + 1 tbsp (75 ml) coconut nectar

1 tbsp (15 ml) fresh lemon juice

3 drops food-grade lavender essential oil

4 drops vanilla extract, Medicine Flower brand preferred

80 g chopped cacao butter, melted

Truffle Coatings

1 batch Enrobing Dark Chocolate (page 156)

1 batch Candied Cacao Nibs (page 152)

½ cup (42.5 g) fine-shred unsweetened dried coconut

2 tbsp (18 g) freeze-dried berry powder (blueberry or açai)

BUCKWHEAT CRUNCH CHOCOLATE BARS WITH APRICOT JAM

Chocolate bars are one of my favorite recipes to make because you get to enjoy so many textures in one bite. The base of this chocolate bar is crunchy like a granola bar (and makes a great snack on its own), and is paired with a gooey apricot jam and topped with a creamy orange layer. These are enrobed in textured dark chocolate with Sprouted and Dehydrated Buckwheat (page 29), so make sure to have some ready before starting this recipe.

Yield: About 30 chocolate bars

CRUNCHY BUCKWHEAT BASE

Make the candied cacao nibs and set aside. In a food processor, process the almonds, coconut flakes, buckwheat, coconut sugar, ground flax, mesquite powder (if using) and salt together until a coarse flour forms. The result should have a lot of texture, so be careful not to overprocess.

Add the apricots, almond butter, coconut nectar, orange zest and vanilla, and process again until combined and the mixture starts sticking together. Last, add the prepared cacao nibs and pulse until incorporated. Line an 8-inch (20-cm) square baking pan with parchment paper and, using your hands, press the crunchy buckwheat base into the bottom of the pan, creating an even layer. Using the back of a spoon, firmly smooth out the layer and set the pan aside while you make the apricot jam.

APRICOT JAM

In a mini or regular food processor (cleaned first if used for the base), process the soaked apricots, coconut nectar, cinnamon and salt until the mixture resembles a thick jam. Using an offset spatula, evenly spread the jam on top of the crunchy buckwheat base. Set aside at room temperature while you make the orange vanilla cream.

(continued)

Crunchy Buckwheat Base

⅓ cup (41 g) Candied Cacao Nibs (page 152)

½ cup (65 g) soaked and dehydrated almonds (see Prep Notes on page 20)

½ cup (32.5 g) large flake unsweetened dried coconut

¼ cup + 2 tbsp (49 g) Sprouted and Dehydrated Buckwheat (page 29)

2 tbsp (20 g) coconut sugar

1 tbsp (7 g) ground golden flax (see Prep Notes on page 18)

1 tbsp (8 g) mesquite powder (optional)

⅛ tsp Himalayan salt

½ cup packed (70 g) dried apricots, soaked for 20 minutes, drained and chopped

2 tbsp (32 g) almond butter

1 tbsp (15 ml) coconut nectar

2 tsp (4 g) orange zest

5 drops vanilla extract, Medicine Flower brand preferred

Apricot Jam

1 cup packed (135 g) dried apricots, soaked for 20 minutes, drained and chopped

2 tbsp (30 ml) coconut nectar

½ tsp ground cinnamon

⅛ tsp Himalayan salt

BUCKWHEAT CRUNCH CHOCOLATE BARS WITH APRICOT JAM (continued)

ORANGE VANILLA CREAM

In a high-speed blender, blend together the cashews, almond milk, coconut nectar, sunflower lecithin, orange zest, vanilla and salt until smooth. Add the melted coconut oil and blend again until well incorporated. Pour the mixture on top of the apricot jam layer and move the pan around from side to side, covering the apricot jam and creating an even layer. Lightly pat the pan on the counter to remove any air bubbles.

Transfer the baking pan to the freezer to chill for a minimum of 8 hours or overnight, until firm. The layers need to be fully frozen to slice into bars.

ASSEMBLY

Remove the pan from the freezer and trim the edges with a knife to create a clean line on all four sides. Slice into 2 x 1–inch (5 x 2.5–cm) bars (you can use a ruler to mark each cut with a knife). Make sure to clean your knife in between each slice. Line a cutting board or tray with parchment paper and transfer the bars to the prepared surface. Place them back in the freezer to firm up and cool before enrobing.

Make or melt the enrobing dark chocolate and transfer it to a small bowl. Add the sprouted and dehydrated buckwheat and mix until incorporated. Remove the bars from the freezer and, using a chocolate dipping fork or regular dinner fork, dip a bar into the melted chocolate for a few seconds with the base facing down. Remove the bar from the chocolate and allow the excess chocolate to drip off. Transfer the enrobed chocolate bar to the lined surface and repeat the process until each bar is enrobed.

Place the bars back in the fridge for 10 minutes to set before serving. They will keep in the fridge for 1 week in a sealed container or the freezer for up to 1 month. They store better in the fridge, as the freezer will create condensation when thawing.

PRO TIP: Make sure the sprouted and dehydrated buckwheat is at room temperature before adding it to the chocolate. If you store yours in the freezer, adding it to the chocolate when it's cold will cause the chocolate to set.

Orange Vanilla Cream

1 cup (140 g) raw cashews, soaked for 2 hours and rinsed

½ cup (120 ml) Almond Milk (page 24)

¼ cup (60 ml) coconut nectar

1½ tsp (scant 4 g) sunflower lecithin powder

1 tsp orange zest

6 drops vanilla extract, Medicine Flower brand preferred

⅛ tsp Himalayan salt

¼ cup (60 ml) melted virgin coconut oil

Assembly

2 batches Enrobing Dark Chocolate (page 156)

½ cup (65 g) Sprouted and Dehydrated Buckwheat (page 29)

MEXICAN CHOCOLATE MOUSSE BARS

These chocolate bars are full of flavors found in Mexican chocolate cake: cinnamon, cayenne and cloves. The base is made from buckwheat and almonds, providing a crunchy texture, and topped with an avocado chocolate mousse. They are delightful once they are cut into bars and enrobed in chocolate! The avocado mousse is a wonderful recipe that can be enjoyed on its own, too.

Yield: About 30 chocolate bars

BLOND BUCKWHEAT CRUNCH BASE

In a food processor, process the almonds, buckwheat, activated oat flour, coconut sugar, mesquite powder and cinnamon until the mixture resembles coarse flour. Add the melted coconut oil, tahini and vanilla, and process again until the batter starts sticking together.

Line an 8-inch (20-cm) square baking pan with parchment paper and, using your hands, press the blond buckwheat crunch base into the bottom of the pan, creating an even layer. Using the back of a spoon, firmly smooth out the layer and set it aside while you make the Mexican chocolate mousse.

MEXICAN CHOCOLATE MOUSSE

In a food processor, process the avocados, cacao powder, coconut milk, coconut nectar, vanilla, cinnamon, salt, cloves and cayenne pepper together until the mixture is smooth. This will take a couple of minutes and you will need to scrape down the sides of the processor. Add the melted coconut oil and process again until the mixture is well combined.

Transfer the mixture to the square pan, on top of the crust, and even out the layer using an offset spatula. Chill the pan in the freezer for 8 hours or overnight, until firm.

(continued)

Blond Buckwheat Crunch Base

1½ cups (195 g) soaked and dehydrated almonds (see Prep Notes on page 20)

½ cup (65 g) Sprouted and Dehydrated Buckwheat (page 29)

½ cup (65 g) Activated Oat Flour (page 28)

¼ cup (40 g) coconut sugar

2 tbsp (16 g) mesquite powder

1 tsp ground cinnamon

¼ cup (60 ml) melted virgin coconut oil

2 tbsp (30 g) tahini

12 drops vanilla extract, Medicine Flower brand preferred

Mexican Chocolate Mousse

2 cups (300 g) peeled, pitted and chopped ripe avocado (about 3 small avocados)

¾ cup (72 g) cacao powder

½ cup (120 ml) Coconut Milk (page 27)

⅔ cup (160 ml) coconut nectar

8 drops vanilla extract, Medicine Flower brand preferred

2 tsp (4.5 g) ground cinnamon

⅛ tsp Himalayan salt

Pinch of ground cloves

⅛ tsp cayenne pepper

¼ cup (60 ml) melted virgin coconut oil

MEXICAN CHOCOLATE
MOUSSE BARS (continued)

ASSEMBLY

Remove the pan from the freezer and trim the edges with a knife to create a clean line on all four sides. Slice into 2 x 1-inch (5 x 2.5-cm) bars (you can use a ruler to mark each cut with a knife). Make sure to clean your knife in between each slice. Line a cutting board or tray with parchment paper and transfer the bars to the prepared surface. Place them back in the freezer for a few hours to firm up and cool before enrobing.

Make or melt the enrobing dark chocolate and transfer the melted chocolate to a small bowl. Remove the bars from the freezer and, using a chocolate dipping fork or regular dinner fork, dip a bar into the melted chocolate for a few seconds with the base facing down (the chocolate mousse layer should be facing up). Remove the bar from the chocolate and allow the excess chocolate to drip off. Transfer the enrobed chocolate bar to the lined surface and repeat the process until each bar is enrobed.

Place the bars back in the fridge for 10 minutes to set before serving. They will keep in the fridge for 1 week in a sealed container or in the freezer for up to 1 month. They store better in the fridge, as the freezer will create condensation when thawing.

Assembly

2 batches Enrobing Dark Chocolate (page 156)

DELECTABLE CAKES

Who doesn't love a beautiful cake? Raw cakes are my jam; I love making them, which is why this chapter has the most recipes. There is nothing more satisfying than creating a beautiful, healthy, homemade cake. There is always an occasion to eat cake, but of course, it can still be enjoyed at any time.

Raw cheesecakes are probably one of the most popular recipes in the raw dessert world, but you will find these cheesecake recipes to be unique and delicious. There are recipes for cultured cheesecakes, fruity cheesecakes, coffee cheesecake and caramel cheesecake with components such as dehydrated jam, caramelized apples and more. If you're a coffee and chocolate lover like me, wait until you try the Mocha Crisp Cheesecake (page 64). This is probably my favorite recipe, and it's the simplest in this chapter.

Believe it or not, you can also create fluffy layered cakes that are completely raw with cakey layers that resemble a baked cake. Carrot cake is probably the most popular flavor, and there is a recipe for that (page 76) with orange cheesecake frosting. Instead of creating a traditional tiramisu recipe, I wanted to do something totally unique, and I created a Three-Layer Tiramisu Cake (page 81). You have to try all the cakes in this chapter; they are one of a kind and delicious!

STRAWBERRY VANILLA CHEESECAKE

Culturing at home is simple, and you will see how easy it is with this cultured cashew cheesecake. This cheesecake has many layers, making it exciting and fun. You will also get to work with agar to create a strawberry vegan gelatin layer on top. Make sure to first prepare the Cultured Cashew Filling (page 30).

Yield: Two 4½-inch (11.5-cm) cakes

COCONUT OAT CRUST

In a food processor, process the coconut, activated oat flour, powdered coconut sugar, mesquite powder (if using) and salt together until the mixture resembles coarse flour.

Add the melted coconut oil, water, lemon zest and vanilla, and process until the batter starts sticking together. Perform a "squeeze test" by taking some of the batter and squeezing it in your hands—if the batter stays formed, it's done.

Line two 4½-inch (11.5-cm) springform pans with parchment paper or plastic wrap on only the removable bottom. Press the crust mixture firmly into the bottom of the pans with your fingers and use the back of a little spoon to even out the crusts. Set aside while you make the strawberry layer.

STRAWBERRY LAYER

In a blender, blend together the cultured cashew filling, filtered water, coconut nectar, freeze-dried strawberries, lemon juice, sunflower lecithin (if using), strawberry extract (if using) and beet powder until smooth. Add the melted coconut oil and blend again until well combined.

Pour the strawberry filling on top of each crust to about 1 inch (2.5 cm) thick and gently pat the cake pan on the counter to remove any air bubbles. Place the extra filling in a container and chill in the fridge to use as a piping garnish. Chill the strawberry layer in the freezer for a minimum of 1 hour before adding the vanilla layer.

(continued)

Coconut Oat Crust

¾ cup (60 g) medium-shred unsweetened dried coconut

¼ cup (33 g) Activated Oat Flour (page 28)

2 tbsp (18 g) powdered coconut sugar (see Prep Notes on page 18)

2 tbsp (16 g) mesquite powder (optional)

⅛ tsp Himalayan salt

2 tbsp (30 ml) melted virgin coconut oil

1 tbsp (15 ml) water

1 tsp fresh lemon zest

3 drops vanilla extract, Medicine Flower brand preferred

Strawberry Layer

1 cup (240 ml) Cultured Cashew Filling (page 30)

½ cup (120 ml) filtered water

¼ cup (60 ml) coconut nectar

¼ cup (9 g) freeze-dried sliced strawberries

1 tbsp (15 ml) fresh lemon juice

1½ tsp (scant 4 g) sunflower lecithin powder (optional)

8 drops strawberry extract, Medicine Flower brand preferred (optional, for a boost of flavor)

½ tsp beet powder (for color)

¼ cup + 2 tbsp (90 ml) melted virgin coconut oil

STRAWBERRY VANILLA CHEESECAKE (continued)

VANILLA LAYER

In a blender, blend together the cultured cashew filling, filtered water, coconut nectar, lemon juice, sunflower lecithin (if using) and vanilla until smooth. Add the melted coconut oil and blend again until well combined.

Pour the vanilla filling on top of each strawberry layer to about 1 inch (2.5 cm) thick and gently pat the cake pan on the counter to remove any air bubbles. Place the extra filling in a container and chill in the fridge to use as a piping garnish. Chill the cheesecakes in the freezer for a minimum of 1 hour before adding the strawberry jelly layer.

STRAWBERRY JELLY

In a blender, blend together the strawberries, water and coconut nectar until smooth. Transfer the mixture to a small pot placed over medium heat and add the agar powder. It is important to heat these ingredients together. Bring the mixture to a boil, then lower the temperature to low and cook for 2 minutes, whisking until the mixture thickens and the agar dissolves. The mixture will darken when the agar is dissolved, then it's ready to use.

Working quickly, pour the strawberry jelly on top of the vanilla layer on each cake, filling to just under the top of the springform pan. Chill the cakes in the freezer for a minimum of 8 hours or overnight, until firm.

ASSEMBLY

Remove the cakes from their springform pans while still frozen and allow them to thaw at room temperature for 30 minutes. While the cakes are thawing, remove the reserved fillings from the fridge to soften. Before piping, slice each thawed cake into eight equal-sized wedges.

You can use either all strawberry filling, all vanilla filling or a combination of both to decorate your cake. The choice is yours. Fit a Wilton® 104 piping tip or an Ateco 125 piping tip to a piping bag and fill the piping bag with your choice of either vanilla or strawberry filling, or both. If you choose to use both, it creates a lovely swirl effect. Spread the filling on one side of the piping bag and spread the other side of the piping bag with the other filling. Above each slice of cake, hold the piping bag horizontally, so the piping tip is in a vertical position with the wide angle of the tip at the bottom. Squeeze the piping bag slowly and, with even pressure, create a ribbon effect on top of each slice of cake.

Top each piped topper with a fresh strawberry, microgreens (if using) and edible gold flake (if using). Serve immediately or store in the fridge for 5 days or in the freezer for up to 1 month. Do not store with the fresh garnishes; add those only when serving.

Vanilla Layer
1 cup (240 ml) Cultured Cashew Filling (page 30)
¼ cup (60 ml) filtered water
¼ cup (60 ml) coconut nectar
1 tbsp (15 ml) fresh lemon juice
1½ tsp (scant 4 g) sunflower lecithin powder (optional)
10 drops vanilla extract, Medicine Flower brand preferred
¼ cup + 2 tbsp (90 ml) melted virgin coconut oil

Strawberry Jelly
1 cup (149 g) frozen strawberries, thawed (measured before thawing)
2 tbsp (30 ml) water
2 tbsp (30 ml) coconut nectar
¾ tsp agar powder

Assembly
Fresh strawberries, cut in half
Microgreens (optional)
Edible gold flake (optional)

RASPBERRY WHITE CHOCOLATE CHEESECAKE

This recipe was inspired by one of my dear friends, a chef, whose favorite dessert flavor combination is raspberry and white chocolate. This cake has two cheese-cake layers, finished with a stunning marbled decoration and a raspberry frosting. Sunflower lecithin powder is optional in some cheesecakes, but does make a difference in the consistency and firmness of the cake. In this recipe, we use light-amber agave as the liquid sweetener to keep the layers light in color, but check out the Substitutions List (page 160) for other alternatives.

Yield: Two 4½-inch (11.5-cm) cakes

RASPBERRY FROSTING

In a high-speed blender, blend together the cashews, raspberries, almond milk, agave, lemon juice and sunflower lecithin (if using) until smooth. Add the mel-ted coconut oil and blend again until well combined. Transfer the frosting to a shallow container and chill in the fridge for 8 hours while you make the rest of the components.

BERRY LEMON CRUST

In a food processor, process the coconut, freeze-dried raspberries, coconut sugar and salt together until the mixture resembles coarse flour. Add the almonds, agave, lemon juice, lemon zest, melted coconut oil and vanilla, and process again for a few seconds until incorporated and the crust starts sticking together. We add the almonds here second so they are coarse and add texture to the crust.

Line two 4½-inch (11.5-cm) springform pans with parchment paper or plastic wrap on just the removable bottom. Press the crust mixture firmly into the bottom of the pans with your fingers and use the back of a little spoon to even out each crust. Set the crusts aside while you make the raspberry ginger filling. If you have leftover crust, it makes a great snack; roll into energy balls and chill them in the fridge.

(continued)

Raspberry Frosting

¼ cup + 2 tbsp (52.5 g) raw cashews, soaked for 2 hours and rinsed

¼ cup + 2 tbsp (46 g) fresh or frozen raspberries (if using frozen, measure after thawed and drained)

2 tbsp (30 ml) Almond Milk (page 24)

2 tbsp (43 ml) light-amber agave

1½ tsp (8 ml) fresh lemon juice

1½ tsp (scant 4 g) sunflower lecithin powder (optional)

¼ cup (60 ml) melted virgin coconut oil

Berry Lemon Crust

¾ cup (60 g) medium-shred unsweetened dried coconut

¼ cup (7 g) freeze-dried raspberries

¼ cup (36 g) powdered coconut sugar (see Prep Notes on page 18)

⅛ tsp Himalayan salt

¾ cup (97.5 g) soaked and dehydrated almonds (see Prep Notes on page 20)

2 tbsp (43 ml) light-amber agave

1 tbsp (15 ml) fresh lemon juice

1 tsp lemon zest

1 tbsp (15 ml) melted virgin coconut oil

8 drops vanilla extract, Medicine Flower brand preferred

RASPBERRY GINGER FILLING

In a high-speed blender, blend together the cashews, raspberries, almond milk, agave, lemon juice, sunflower lecithin (if using) and ginger until smooth. Add the melted coconut oil and blend again until well combined.

Pour the raspberry ginger filling on top of each crust to about ⅜ inch (1 cm) thick, reserving a small amount to create a marbled decoration on top later. I use a butter knife to measure by dipping it into the filling and gauging the height. Gently pat the pans on the counter to remove any air bubbles and chill in the freezer for a few hours, until the layer is firm enough to add the next layer.

WHITE CHOCOLATE FILLING

In a high-speed blender, blend together the cashews, almond milk, agave, sunflower lecithin (if using) and vanilla until smooth. Add the melted cacao butter and blend again until well combined. Pour the white chocolate filling on top of the raspberry ginger filling in each pan to about ⅜ inch (1 cm) thick. I use a butter knife to measure by dipping it into the filling and gauging the height.

Gently pat the pans on the counter to remove any air bubbles. Transfer the leftover raspberry ginger filling to a squeeze bottle or piping bag with the end cut off to create a small hole (if the filling has set, melt it down until it's liquid). Create dots on top of the cake in a circular pattern starting from the middle, working your way to the outer edges. Using a toothpick or wooden skewer, only grazing the top, create a marble effect.

Chill the cakes in the freezer for a minimum of 8 hours or overnight, until firm. The cakes need to be frozen to smoothly remove them from the springform pans.

ASSEMBLY

Remove the cakes from their springform pans while still frozen and allow them to thaw at room temperature for 30 minutes. While the cakes are thawing, remove the raspberry frosting from the fridge to soften.

Fit a Wilton 1M piping tip to a piping bag and fill the piping bag with the raspberry frosting. Hold the piping bag with the tip down vertical to the cake and create dollops of frosting on top of the cake toward the outer edges until you've created a full ring.

Garnish with edible flowers (if using), microgreens (if using) and fresh raspberries. Serve immediately or store in the fridge for 5 days or in the freezer for up to 1 month. Do not store with microgreens and edible flowers; add just before serving.

Raspberry Ginger Filling

¾ cup (105 g) raw cashews, soaked for 2 hours and rinsed

¾ cup (94 g) fresh or frozen raspberries (if using frozen, measure after thawed and drained)

¼ cup (60 ml) Almond Milk (page 24)

¼ cup (85 g) light-amber agave

1 tbsp (15 ml) fresh lemon juice

1½ tsp (scant 4 g) sunflower lecithin powder (optional)

1 tsp grated fresh ginger

¼ cup (60 ml) melted virgin coconut oil

White Chocolate Filling

1 cup (140 g) raw cashews, soaked for 2 hours and rinsed

½ cup (120 ml) Almond Milk (page 24)

¼ cup (85 g) light-amber agave

1½ tsp (scant 4 g) sunflower lecithin powder (optional)

6 drops vanilla extract, Medicine Flower brand preferred

¼ cup (50 g) chopped and melted cacao butter

Assembly

Edible flowers (optional)

Microgreens (optional)

Fresh raspberries

APPLE CRUMBLE CARAMEL CHEESECAKE

This cultured caramel cheesecake is full of fall flavors and spices. If you're a fan of apple pie, you will love this twist on a cheesecake. Make sure to have a batch of the Cultured Cashew Filling (page 30) prepared; I recommend prepping the filling while the spiced walnut oat crumble is in the dehydrator. The oat crumble topping is also an excellent recipe on its own and is great as granola or cereal!

Yield: Two 4½-inch (11.5-cm) cakes

SPICED WALNUT OAT CRUMBLE

In a food processor, process the walnuts, oats, coconut flakes, coconut nectar, lemon juice, ginger, cinnamon, vanilla, nutmeg, allspice, cardamom and salt together until a crumble forms.

Spread the mixture on a lined dehydrator tray and dehydrate at 115°F (46°C) for 16 to 18 hours, flipping the crumble halfway through. Transfer the crumble to the freezer and let it cool and crisp up. The extra crumble makes wonderful granola and will keep in the freezer for months.

CARAMELIZED APPLES

In a bowl, combine the apples, coconut nectar, coconut sugar, lemon juice, cinnamon, vanilla and salt until well mixed. Place the bowl on the bottom tray of your dehydrator and dehydrate the mixture in the bowl at 115°F (46°C) for 8 to 9 hours, or until the mixture is thick and reduced. Transfer the mixture to a container and store it in the fridge to cool and thicken up until it is ready to use.

(continued)

Spiced Walnut Oat Crumble

1 cup (100 g) raw walnuts, soaked for 4 hours and rinsed

1 cup (80 g) gluten-free rolled oats

¾ cup (49 g) large flake unsweetened dried coconut

¼ cup (60 ml) coconut nectar

1 tbsp (15 ml) fresh lemon juice

1 tsp grated fresh ginger

1 tsp ground cinnamon

12 drops vanilla extract, Medicine Flower brand preferred

⅛ tsp ground nutmeg

⅛ tsp ground allspice

⅛ tsp ground cardamom

⅛ tsp Himalayan salt

Caramelized Apples

4 red apples, unpeeled, cored and small diced

¼ cup + 2 tbsp (90 ml) coconut nectar

2 tbsp (20 g) coconut sugar

1 tbsp (15 ml) fresh lemon juice

1 tsp ground cinnamon

4 drops vanilla extract, Medicine Flower brand preferred

Pinch of Himalayan salt

APPLE CRUMBLE CARAMEL CHEESECAKE (continued)

COCONUT GINGER CRUST

In a food processor, process the shredded coconut, activated oat flour, powdered coconut sugar, mesquite powder and salt together until the mixture resembles coarse flour. Add the melted coconut oil, water, ginger and vanilla, and process until the batter sticks together. Perform a "squeeze test" by taking some of the crust batter and squeezing it in your hands; if the batter stays formed, it's done processing. If it's dry, process it a little longer to release the oils from the shredded coconut.

Line two 4½-inch (11.5-cm) springform pans with parchment paper or plastic wrap on only the removable bottom. Press the crust mixture firmly into the bottom of each pan with your fingers and use the back of a little spoon to even out the crust. Set aside while you make the filling.

CULTURED CARAMEL FILLING

Before making this component, ensure your caramelized apples and spiced walnut oat crumble are done dehydrating. Blend the cultured cashew filling, water, coconut nectar, lemon juice, sunflower lecithin, melted coconut oil, mesquite powder, cinnamon and salt until smooth.

Place some caramelized apples in the center of each cake crust, leaving about ⅜ inch (1 cm) of space around the edges. If you put the caramelized apples too close to the edge of the springform pan, it will be difficult to remove the pan. Reserve some caramelized apples to use as garnish.

Pour the cultured caramel filling into the springform pans, filling them to just below the top of the pans. Take some of the spiced walnut oat crumble and create a layer on top of the filling, pressing the crumble into the filling so the crumble sets into the top of the filling. Chill the cakes in the freezer for a minimum of 8 hours or overnight, until firm.

ASSEMBLY

Remove the cakes from the springform pans while still frozen and allow them to thaw at room temperature for 30 minutes. Slice each cake into eight equal-sized wedges and serve each piece with extra caramelized apples, vanilla bean whip or vanilla bean ice cream and top with an edible flower (if using) and microgreens (if using).

Coconut Ginger Crust

1 cup (80 g) medium-shred unsweetened dried coconut

¼ cup (33 g) Activated Oat Flour (page 28)

2 tbsp (18 g) powdered coconut sugar (see Prep Notes on page 18)

2 tbsp (16 g) mesquite powder

⅛ tsp Himalayan salt

2 tbsp (30 ml) melted virgin coconut oil

1 tbsp (15 ml) water

1 tsp grated fresh ginger

3 drops vanilla extract, Medicine Flower brand preferred

Cultured Caramel Filling

1 cup (240 ml) Cultured Cashew Filling (page 30)

¼ cup (60 ml) water

¼ cup (60 ml) coconut nectar

1½ tsp (8 ml) fresh lemon juice

1½ tsp (scant 4 g) sunflower lecithin powder

¼ cup + 2 tbsp (90 ml) melted virgin coconut oil

1 tbsp (8 g) mesquite powder

½ tsp ground cinnamon

⅛ tsp Himalayan salt

Assembly

Leftover Caramelized Apples

1 batch Vanilla Bean Coconut Whip (page 157) or Vanilla Bean Ice Cream (page 120)

Edible flowers (optional)

Microgreens (optional)

BLACKBERRY GINGER LIME ZEBRA CHEESECAKE

The great thing about zebra cakes is that you can create multiple layers without waiting for each layer to set, since we use multiple fillings at once to create the zebra pattern. So, although this cake may look intimidating, it's actually simple to make; check out the progress photos. Take a look at the Substitutions List (page 160) for dried white mulberry and xylitol alternatives.

Yield: Two 4½-inch (11.5-cm) cakes

MULBERRY ALMOND CRUST

In a food processor, process the almonds, coconut, powdered coconut sugar and lucuma powder together until the mixture resembles coarse flour. Add the soaked mulberries, melted coconut oil, lime zest and ginger, and process again until the batter starts sticking together. Do not overprocess this mixture, or it will be too oily.

Line two 4½-inch (11.5-cm) springform pans with parchment paper or plastic wrap on only the removable bottom. Press the crust mixture firmly into the bottom of the pans with your fingers and use the back of a little spoon to even out the crust. Set aside while you make the fillings. If you have leftover crust, it makes for a great snack; roll into energy balls and chill them in the fridge until firm.

BLACKBERRY GINGER FILLING

In a blender, blend together the cashews, blackberries, almond milk, agave, lemon juice, sunflower lecithin (if using), ginger and salt until smooth. Add the melted coconut oil and blend again until well combined. Transfer the filling to a squeeze bottle or piping bag and set aside while you blend the lime filling.

(continued)

Mulberry Almond Crust

½ cup (65 g) soaked and dehydrated almonds (see Prep Notes on page 20)

½ cup (40 g) medium-shred unsweetened dried coconut

2 tbsp (18 g) powdered coconut sugar (see Prep Notes on page 18)

1 tbsp (7.5 g) lucuma powder

¼ cup (28 g) dried white mulberries, soaked for 20 minutes to soften and drained

2 tbsp (30 ml) melted virgin coconut oil

½ tsp lime zest

½ tsp grated fresh ginger

Blackberry Ginger Filling

¾ cup (105 g) raw cashews, soaked for 2 hours and rinsed

¾ cup (113 g) fresh or frozen blackberries (if using frozen, measure after thawed and drained)

¼ cup (60 ml) Almond Milk (page 24)

2 tbsp (43 ml) light-amber agave

1 tbsp (15 ml) fresh lemon juice

1½ tsp (scant 4 g) sunflower lecithin powder (optional)

1 tsp grated fresh ginger

Small pinch of Himalayan salt

¼ cup (60 ml) melted virgin coconut oil

LIME FILLING

In a blender, blend together the cashews, almond milk, lime juice, agave, sunflower lecithin (if using), matcha powder and salt until smooth. Add the melted coconut oil and blend again until well combined. Transfer the filling to a second squeeze bottle or piping bag.

ASSEMBLY

Starting with the blackberry ginger filling, squeeze about 2 tablespoons (30 ml) onto the center of the crust, creating a circle. Follow with the lime layer, squeezing about 2 tablespoons (30 ml) on top of the blackberry ginger layer, using even pressure on the squeeze bottle or piping bag to spread the layers toward the outer edges of the crust. Repeat this method until both springform pans are full.

Using a toothpick or small knife, marble the top of each cake carefully, only grazing the top. Chill the cakes in the freezer for a minimum of 8 hours or overnight. Remove the cakes from the springform pans while still frozen and allow them to thaw at room temperature for 30 minutes.

Check on the coconut frosting; it should be firm to the touch. If it's not firm, chill it in the freezer for 10 to 20 minutes to firm up, and if it's too firm, allow it to soften at room temperature. Once the frosting is ready for piping, fit a Wilton 1M piping tip to a piping bag and fill the piping bag with the coconut frosting. Hold the piping bag with the tip above a cake vertically and place dollops of frosting on the outside edge of the cake until the entire edge of the cake is covered. Repeat with the other cake.

Garnish with fresh blackberries and microgreens or mint. Serve immediately or store them in the fridge for 5 days or in the freezer for up to 1 month. Do not store with fresh garnishes; add them just before serving.

Lime Filling

1 cup (140 g) raw cashews, soaked for 2 hours and rinsed

¼ cup (60 ml) Almond Milk (page 24)

¼ cup (60 ml) fresh lime juice

2 tbsp (43 ml) light-amber agave

1½ tsp (scant 4 g) sunflower lecithin powder (optional)

½ tsp matcha or moringa powder (for color)

Small pinch of Himalayan salt

¼ cup (60 ml) melted virgin coconut oil

Assembly

1 batch Coconut Frosting (page 148)

Fresh blackberries, sliced

Microgreens or fresh mint

MOCHA CRISP CHEESECAKE

Yield: Two 4½-inch (11.5-cm) cakes

Have you ever had a Coffee Crisp® chocolate bar? This Canadian treat was my favorite chocolate bar as a child. This cheesecake is in my top five of the best desserts I've ever eaten; the crust and filling paired together taste like a Coffee Crisp chocolate bar.

ALMOND ESPRESSO CRUST

In a food processor, process the almonds, buckwheat, activated oat flour, mesquite powder, coconut sugar and espresso powder (if using) together until a coarse flour forms. Do not overprocess these ingredients since texture should be present in the crust. Add the melted coconut oil, almond butter and vanilla, and process again until the mixture starts sticking together.

Line two 4½-inch (11.5-cm) springform pans with parchment paper or plastic wrap on only the removable bottom. Press the crust mixture firmly into the bottom of each pan with your fingers and use the back of a little spoon to even out the crust. Set aside at room temperature while you make the chocolate espresso filling.

CHOCOLATE ESPRESSO FILLING

Before starting the filling, have some white chocolate sauce prepared and ready to use for the next step. In a high-speed blender, blend together the cashews, coffee, cacao powder, coconut nectar, lemon juice, sunflower lecithin, vanilla and salt until combined and smooth. The mixture will be very thick, but it will thin out once you add the cacao butter. Add the melted cacao butter and blend on low speed for a few seconds until well incorporated.

ASSEMBLY

Pour the chocolate espresso filling into each cake pan, filling them to the top. Transfer the white chocolate sauce to a squeeze bottle or piping bag, and on top of the filling, create dots in a circular pattern, starting from the middle, working your way to the outer edges. Using a toothpick or wooden skewer, only grazing the top, create a marbled effect.

In a blender, blitz the cacao nibs to create smaller pieces and place them on the outside edges of the cakes for decoration. Chill the cakes in the freezer for a minimum of 8 hours or overnight, until firm. The cakes need to be frozen to smoothly remove them from the springform pans. Remove the pans from the freezer and remove each cake from its springform pan while still frozen. Allow the cakes to thaw for about 30 minutes at room temperature before slicing. Serve immediately or store in the fridge for 5 days or in the freezer for up to 1 month.

Almond Espresso Crust

¾ cup (97.5 g) soaked and dehydrated almonds (see Prep Notes on page 20)

¼ cup (33 g) Sprouted and Dehydrated Buckwheat (page 29)

¼ cup (33 g) Activated Oat Flour (page 28)

2 tbsp (16 g) mesquite powder

2 tbsp (20 g) coconut sugar

⅛ tsp espresso powder (optional)

2 tbsp (30 ml) melted virgin coconut oil

1 tbsp (16 g) almond butter

6 drops vanilla extract, Medicine Flower brand preferred

Chocolate Espresso Filling

1 cup (140 g) raw cashews, soaked for 2 hours and rinsed

½ cup (120 ml) strongly brewed coffee

¼ cup (24 g) cacao powder

¼ cup (60 ml) coconut nectar

1 tsp fresh lemon juice

1 tsp sunflower lecithin powder

6 drops vanilla extract, Medicine Flower brand preferred

⅛ tsp Himalayan salt

¼ cup (50 g) chopped cacao butter, melted

Assembly

1 batch White Chocolate Sauce (page 158)

¼ cup (30 g) cacao nibs

CHOCOLATE MOUSSE CAKE WITH CHERRY JAM

If you're a chocolate lover, then this cake is for you! Made with nut-free ingredients, this cake is full of texture and explodes with cherry, vanilla and cacao flavors that will win over anyone. If you don't like cherries or cannot source them, any frozen berry will work. Coconut nectar is used to sweeten this cake, but check out the Substitutions List (page 160) for other fun ways to add a natural sweetness.

Yield: Two 4½-inch (11.5-cm) cakes
Nut-free

TART CHERRY JAM

In a food processor, combine the cherries, coconut nectar, black cherry flavor (if using) and salt and pulse until a chunky texture is achieved.

Transfer the mixture to a stainless-steel or glass bowl, place in the bottom or on a lower tray of your dehydrator, and dehydrate at 115°F (46°C) for 18 to 24 hours, or until reduced and thick.

CHOCOLATE COCONUT CRUST

In a food processor, process the coconut, powdered coconut sugar and cacao powder together until the mixture resembles coarse flour. Add the dates, cacao nibs, melted coconut oil, lemon juice and vanilla, and process until the batter starts sticking together. You will know it is ready when the batter starts to form a ball.

Line two 4½-inch (11.5-cm) springform pans with parchment paper or plastic wrap on only the removable bottom and line the inner side of the pan's ring with a cake collar or acetate sheet. Press the crust mixture firmly into the bottom of each pan with your fingers and use the back of a little spoon to even out the crust. Set aside while you make the chocolate mousse filling. If you have leftover crust, it makes a great snack or topping to ice cream, oatmeal, smoothie bowls or cereal!

(continued)

Tart Cherry Jam

2 cups (308 g) frozen tart cherries, thawed (measured before thawing)

⅓ cup (80 ml) coconut nectar

3 drops black cherry extract, Medicine Flower brand preferred (optional, for a boost of flavor)

⅛ tsp Himalayan salt

Chocolate Coconut Crust

1 cup (65 g) large flake unsweetened dried coconut

¼ cup (36 g) powdered coconut sugar (see Prep Notes on page 18)

⅓ cup (32 g) cacao powder

½ cup (89 g) Medjool dates, soaked until softened and pitted (about 5 large dates)

¼ cup (30 g) cacao nibs

2 tbsp (30 ml) melted virgin coconut oil

1 tbsp (15 ml) fresh lemon juice

3 drops vanilla extract, Medicine Flower brand preferred

CHOCOLATE MOUSSE CAKE
WITH CHERRY JAM (continued)

CHOCOLATE MOUSSE

In a blender, blend together the cacao powder, coconut nectar, melted coconut oil, powdered coconut sugar, melted cacao butter, vanilla, salt and cayenne until smooth. While the blender is running on low speed, slowly add the coconut cream and blend only for a few seconds until well incorporated.

ASSEMBLY

Place some cherry jam on the center of each crust, leaving about ⅜ inch (1 cm) of space around the outside edges. This is so the cherry jam won't leak out when cutting the cake. Pour the chocolate mousse into each pan, leaving a ¼-inch (6-mm) headspace to make room for the dark chocolate ganache. Pat the pans on the counter to remove any air bubbles. Chill the cakes in the freezer for a minimum of 2 hours; also, place the extra chocolate mousse in a container and chill it in the fridge until the cake is finished, to use as a piping garnish.

Once the cakes have chilled in the freezer and the chocolate mousse is firm to the touch, top the cakes with the dark chocolate ganache, filling to the top of the cake pans. Chill the cakes in the freezer overnight or for a minimum of 6 hours, until firm. Remove the leftover chocolate mousse filling from the fridge. If it is too firm, let it sit at room temperature for 30 minutes to an hour to soften. Remove the cakes from their springform pan while still frozen and remove the cake collars from the outside of each cake. Allow the cakes to thaw at room temperature for 30 minutes. Slice each cake into eight equal-sized wedges.

Fit a Wilton 1M piping tip to a piping bag and fill the piping bag with the leftover chocolate mousse. Holding the piping bag vertically above a slice of cake, squeeze the bag slowly with even pressure to create a dollop of chocolate mousse filling on top of the slice. Repeat this method on each slice of cake.

Top with a cherry. Serve immediately or store in a sealed container in the freezer for up to 1 month.

PRO TIPS: Be patient when adding the coconut cream to the chocolate mousse. If it starts to look grainy, blend a little longer until the filling is smooth.

A cake collar or acetate sheet is required for cakes topped with the dark chocolate ganache; otherwise, they will stick to the springform pan.

Chocolate Mousse
½ cup (48 g) cacao powder

½ cup (120 ml) coconut nectar

½ cup (120 ml) melted virgin coconut oil

¼ cup (36 g) powdered coconut sugar (see Prep Notes on page 18)

¼ cup (50 g) chopped and melted cacao butter

8 drops vanilla extract, Medicine Flower brand preferred

⅛ tsp Himalayan salt

Small pinch of cayenne pepper

½ cup (120 ml) Coconut Cream (page 27)

Assembly
½ batch Dark Chocolate Ganache (page 153)

8 cherries, fresh or frozen and thawed

TROPICAL LIME COCONUT ENTREMETS

Yield: Three 2-inch (5-cm) square mini cakes
Nut-free

These stunning, nut-free, tropical lime cakes may look intimidating, but they are simpler to make than you would think. They're paired with a textured mulberry crust, creamy lime coconut filling, mango pineapple jelly center and finished with a white chocolate and lime glaze. Decorating these are a lot of fun and a great recipe to wow your dinner guests with. This recipe uses young coconut meat, but check out the Substitutions List (page 160) for other options.

MULBERRY COCONUT CRUST

In a food processor, process the shredded coconut, coconut sugar and salt together until the mixture resembles coarse flour. Add the mulberries, coconut butter, lime zest and vanilla, and process until the batter starts sticking together.

Secure a piece of parchment paper or a reusable dehydrator liner on a countertop and remove the batter from the food processor, forming it into a ball on the parchment. Place another piece of parchment on top of the batter. Using a rolling pin, roll out the batter to about ¼ inch (6 mm) thick. Use a 2.5-inch (6.5-cm) square cookie cutter to form square bases for the cake. Remove the square bases with an offset spatula and place them on a lined tray or cutting board. Repeat the process until all the batter is used. This recipe makes about six crusts. Set the crusts in the freezer until all the other components are ready.

MANGO PINEAPPLE JELLY

In a blender, blend together the thawed mango and pineapple until smooth. Strain the mixture through a nut milk bag into a bowl; the mixture will be thick like a puree and should yield about 1 cup (240 ml).

Place the puree, agave, agar powder and salt in a pot and bring to a boil over medium heat for 2 minutes, stirring constantly with a whisk. Lower the temperature to low and keep whisking until the cloudy texture has disappeared; this is how you know it's ready. Transfer the mixture to a liquid measuring cup and place a sphere mold with 1.5-inch (4-cm) cavities on a cutting board or tray. Carefully pour the mixture into the silicone mold; it should fill up 12 cavities. Transfer to the freezer and let set for a minimum of 6 hours.

When the jelly is firm enough to remove from the silicone mold, place two half-spheres together, creating a full sphere. This will be placed inside the cake's filling as the center. Because the jelly is sticky, the two halves should stick together easily.

Mulberry Coconut Crust

1 cup (80 g) medium-shred unsweetened dried coconut

¼ cup (40 g) coconut sugar

⅛ tsp Himalayan salt

½ cup (56 g) dried white mulberries, soaked for 20 minutes

2 tbsp (30 g) softened Coconut Butter (page 31)

1 tsp lime zest

3 drops vanilla extract, Medicine Flower brand preferred

Mango Pineapple Jelly

1½ cups (225 g) frozen mango, thawed (measured before thawing)

1 cup (135 g) frozen pineapple, thawed (measured before thawing)

2 tbsp (43 ml) light-amber agave

¾ tsp agar powder

Pinch of Himalayan salt

(continued)

LIME COCONUT CREAM FILLING

In a high-speed blender, blend together the coconut meat, agave, lime juice, coconut milk, sunflower lecithin, vanilla and salt until smooth. If the mixture is quite thick, add a little more coconut milk to help it blend. If you are using the vanilla bean, slice it open down the middle and remove the seeds with the tip of your knife by scraping the bean. Add them to the blender and blend again on low speed for a few seconds to incorporate them.

Add the coconut butter and blend until well incorporated. If any of the ingredients are cold, they may start setting in the blender when you add the coconut butter and look curdled. If this happens, keep blending until the mixture warms and looks smooth.

Place a square silicone mold with 2-inch (5-cm) cavities onto a cutting board or tray. Pour the filling into three cavities, filling each about three-quarters full. Take one full sphere of jelly and place it into the middle of each cavity of filling, pressing it down gently and making sure not to press it into the bottom. Fill the three cavities the rest of the way with the lime coconut cream filling.

Tap the mold lightly to remove any air bubbles and place in the freezer to set for 8 hours or overnight. Remove the cakes from the mold and place them on a tray in the freezer for a few hours before glazing.

WHITE CHOCOLATE LIME GLAZE

Only make the white chocolate lime glaze when you're ready to assemble the cakes, as you need to use it right away. The cakes should be removed from the mold and already in the freezer for a few hours to ensure they are frozen and prepped for the glaze.

In a high-speed blender, blend together the melted cacao butter, coconut milk, coconut butter, xylitol, agave, lime juice, vanilla and salt. If any of the ingredients are cold, the cacao butter and coconut butter will start to set. If this happens, keep blending until the mixture is warm and everything incorporates and looks smooth.

(continued)

Lime Coconut Cream Filling

1 cup (160 g) chopped young coconut meat

¼ cup (85 g) light-amber agave

¼ cup (60 ml) fresh lime juice

¼ cup (60 ml) Coconut Milk (page 27), plus more as needed

1½ tsp (scant 4 g) sunflower lecithin powder

6 drops vanilla extract, Medicine Flower brand preferred, or seeds from ½ vanilla bean

⅛ tsp Himalayan salt

¼ cup (60 g) softened Coconut Butter (page 31)

White Chocolate Lime Glaze

½ cup + 2 tbsp (125 g) chopped and melted cacao butter

⅓ cup (80 ml) Coconut Milk (page 27)

¼ cup + 2 tbsp (90 g) softened Coconut Butter (page 31)

¼ cup (49 g) powdered xylitol (see Prep Notes on page 18)

2 tbsp (43 ml) light-amber agave

1 tbsp (15 ml) fresh lime juice

6 drops vanilla extract, Medicine Flower brand preferred

Pinch of Himalayan salt

TROPICAL LIME COCONUT ENTREMETS (continued)

ASSEMBLY

Remove the crusts from the freezer and trim the edges a tiny bit to clean them up. For this recipe, it would be good to gather your tools before you start assembling: You will need a cooling rack, baking sheet, wooden skewer or large toothpick and a cutting board or tray for glazing; also, have some fine shredded coconut ready on a plate. Place the cooling rack on top of the baking sheet, place one cake on the cooling rack and pour the glaze from the blender over the top of the cake from each edge to the middle, ensuring coverage of the entire cake.

Using a wooden skewer, firmly pierce the top of the cake in the middle and use it to remove the cake from the cooling rack so you don't mess up the glaze from transferring it. Dip the bottom of the cake into the coconut, ensuring the bottom edges are covered. Place the cake on top of a crust and set it aside while finishing the other two cakes. Repeat the same process until the rest of the cakes are done and prep your piping bag for decoration.

Fit a Wilton 104 piping tip to a piping bag and fill the piping bag with the vanilla bean coconut whip. Above a slice of cake, hold the piping bag horizontally, so the piping tip is in a vertical position with the wide angle at the bottom and create a ribbon effect from one corner to the opposite corner.

Garnish with mint, edible flowers (if using) and more fine shredded coconut. Serve immediately or store in the freezer without the fresh garnishes for up to 1 month or in the fridge for up to 3 days.

Assembly

¼ cup (21 g) fine-shred unsweetened dried coconut

1 batch Vanilla Bean Coconut Whip (page 157) or ½ batch Coconut Frosting (page 148)

Fresh mint leaves

Edible flowers (optional)

APRICOT PECAN BUTTERNUT SQUASH CAKE WITH COCONUT CREAM

Butternut squash is a wonderful ingredient to use in desserts, replacing the need for nuts; and yes, you can eat it raw! The butternut cream filling tastes just like traditional pumpkin pie but is better and full of nutritional value. These cakes must be thawed in the fridge so both fillings are the same consistency. If you cannot source butternut squash, check out the Substitutions List (page 160) for other options.

Yield: Two 4½-inch (11.5-cm) cakes

CANDIED PECAN CRUMBLE

In a food processor, pulse the pecans, coconut sugar, coconut nectar, cinnamon and salt together until a crumble forms and the ingredients are combined. Spread the pecan crumble on a lined dehydrator tray and dehydrate at 115°F (46°C) for 18 to 20 hours. Transfer to an open container and place the crumble in the freezer to crisp up and cool. It will feel sticky when warm, but once cooled, it will crisp up. Store in the freezer until it's ready to use.

APRICOT PECAN GINGER CRUST

In a food processor, process the pecans, coconut, coconut sugar, mesquite powder and salt together until the mixture resembles coarse flour. Add the soaked apricots, melted coconut oil, ginger and vanilla, and process again until combined and the crust starts sticking together.

Line two 4½-inch (11.5-cm) springform pans with parchment paper or plastic wrap on only the removable bottom. Line the inner side of the pan's ring with an acetate sheet or cake collar, then press the crust mixture firmly into the bottom of each pan with your fingers and use the back of a little spoon to even out each crust. Set aside while you make the butternut squash cream filling. If you have crust leftover, it makes a great snack; roll into energy balls and chill them in the fridge.

(continued)

Candied Pecan Crumble

1 cup (100 g) pecans, soaked for 4 hours and rinsed

2 tbsp (20 g) coconut sugar

1 tbsp (15 ml) coconut nectar

1 tsp ground cinnamon

⅛ tsp Himalayan salt

Apricot Pecan Ginger Crust

¾ cup (82 g) soaked and dehydrated pecans (see Prep Notes on page 20)

½ cup (40 g) medium-shred unsweetened dried coconut

¼ cup (40 g) coconut sugar

1 tbsp (8 g) mesquite powder

⅛ tsp Himalayan salt

½ cup (65 g) dried apricots, soaked for 20 minutes, drained and chopped

1 tbsp (15 ml) melted virgin coconut oil

1 tsp grated fresh ginger

3 drops vanilla extract, Medicine Flower brand preferred

BUTTERNUT SQUASH CREAM FILLING

In a blender, blend together the butternut squash, coconut milk, coconut sugar, roasted tahini, sunflower lecithin, pumpkin pie spice and cinnamon until combined. The mixture will not be entirely smooth as the butternut squash will produce some graininess. Add the melted cacao butter and blend on low speed until incorporated.

Pour the butternut squash cream filling on top of each crust, filling each springform pan three-quarters full, leaving room for the coconut cream layer. Gently pat the pans on the counter to remove any air bubbles and chill in the freezer for a few hours, or until the layer is firm enough to add the coconut cream layer.

COCONUT CREAM LAYER

In a blender, blend together the coconut milk, coconut butter, agave, lemon juice, melted coconut oil and sunflower lecithin until smooth. The mixture will start to set and will look grainy in the blender if the coconut milk is cold. If that happens, keep blending the mixture to warm it up until it's smooth. Pour the coconut cream layer on top of the butternut squash cream filling and gently pat the springform pans on the counter to remove any air bubbles.

ASSEMBLY

Remove the candied pecan crumble from the freezer and transfer to a small bowl. Using a small spoon, scoop some pecan crumble and place it along the circumference of each cake, gently pressing the crumble into the coconut cream layer. Work fast as the coconut cream layer will start setting quickly. Chill the cakes in the freezer for a minimum of 8 hours or overnight.

Remove the cakes from the freezer, remove the springform pans and cake collars and thaw the cakes in the fridge overnight before serving. This cake is best thawed in the fridge overnight rather than thawed at room temperature. Remove from the fridge, slice and serve immediately. This cake will store in the freezer for up to 1 month or the fridge for 5 days.

PRO TIPS: Peel the butternut squash first with a vegetable peeler, cut it in half and remove the seeds before chopping into cubes.

We use a cake collar or acetate sheet for this cake because the coconut cream layer is soft and will stick to the sides of the pans.

Butternut Squash Cream Filling

1½ cups (225 g) peeled, seeded and cubed butternut squash (see Pro Tip)

¼ cup (60 ml) Coconut Milk (page 27)

¼ cup + 2 tbsp (60 g) coconut sugar

2 tbsp (30 g) roasted tahini

1½ tsp (scant 4 g) sunflower lecithin powder

1 tsp pumpkin pie spice

½ tsp ground cinnamon

¼ cup (50 g) chopped and melted cacao butter

Coconut Cream Layer

¼ cup + 1 tbsp (75 ml) Coconut Milk (page 27)

¼ cup (60 g) softened Coconut Butter (page 31)

¼ cup (85 g) light-amber agave

1 tbsp (15 ml) fresh lemon juice

1 tbsp (15 ml) melted virgin coconut oil

1 tsp sunflower lecithin powder

CARROT CAKE WITH ORANGE CHEESECAKE FROSTING

Yield: One three-layer 4½-inch (11.5-cm) cake

Carrot cake makes my heart sing because any dessert with veggies is a score! This one is unique, thanks to the dehydrated cake bases. Make sure you have some Coconut Frosting (page 148) prepared for this recipe to use as a garnish on top of the cake. The spiced walnut crumble is optional but adds a nice decoration on the bottom of the cake and more texture. For frosting the cake, you will need cake decorating tools, such as piping bags, an offset spatula, a pastry scraper (optional), a cake board and a cake turntable (optional). Check out the progress photos for the Three-Layer Tiramisu Cake (page 81) for putting this three-layer cake together.

SPICED WALNUT CRUMBLE

If you are making the spiced crumble, in a food processor, process the walnuts, coconut sugar and cinnamon together to form a crumble. Spread on a lined dehydrator tray and dehydrate at 115°F (46°C) for 18 to 24 hours. Transfer the mixture to the freezer to cool and crisp up, then process in a food processor to break down into a crumble before use.

ORANGE CHEESECAKE FROSTING

In a blender, blend together the cultured cashew frosting base, xylitol, orange juice and zest, vanilla and orange essential oil (if using) until smooth. You may need your tamper as the mixture will be thick. Add the melted coconut oil and blend again until well combined. Transfer the frosting to a shallow container and place in the fridge for 12 hours or overnight to set while you make the rest of the components.

(continued)

Spiced Walnut Crumble (optional)

1 cup (100 g) raw walnuts, soaked for 4 hours and rinsed

1 tbsp (10 g) coconut sugar

1 tsp ground cinnamon

Orange Cheesecake Frosting

1 batch Cultured Cashew Frosting Base (page 151)

¾ cup (146 g) powdered xylitol (see Prep Notes on page 18)

¼ cup (60 ml) fresh orange juice

1 tsp orange zest

6 drops vanilla extract, Medicine Flower brand preferred

3 drops food-grade orange essential oil (optional, for a boost of flavor)

¾ cup (180 ml) melted virgin coconut oil

CARROT CAKE WITH ORANGE CHEESECAKE FROSTING
(continued)

CARROT CAKE BASES

In a food processor, process the almonds, coconut, coconut flour, ground flax, mesquite powder (if using), psyllium, cinnamon, nutmeg, ground cloves and salt together until the mixture resembles coarse flour. Add the carrots, water, dates, walnuts, coconut nectar, raisins and ginger, and process again until combined. You will have to stop the processor and scrape down the sides a few times. Do not overprocess the mixture; there should be a lot of texture.

Line a tray or cutting board with parchment paper. Remove the bottom of a 4½-inch (11.5-cm) springform pan and clip its ring shut; we will use the ring as a mold for the cake bases. Place the empty ring on the prepared tray, and press the carrot cake base into it, creating a cake layer ½ inch (1.3 cm) thick. Use the back of a small spoon to even out the base and remove it from the springform ring. Repeat this process two more times until you have three separate cake bases on the parchment paper. You will have extra carrot cake base batter; roll it into energy bites and place them in the fridge to firm up to enjoy as a snack.

Transfer the parchment paper with the cake bases to a dehydrator tray and dehydrate at 115°F (46°C) for 1 hour, then flip the cake bases onto a mesh-lined tray. Continue to dehydrate for 7½ hours. The cake bases should still be moist on the inside. Transfer the cake bases to the freezer for 2 hours to cool before frosting.

ASSEMBLY

First, check on your frosting; you need to ensure your frosting is at the perfect consistency for piping. Remove the frosting from the fridge and check to see whether it is firm. If it's really soft, place in the freezer for 10 to 20 minutes, remove from the freezer and stir the frosting, whipping it up. If it's too firm, allow it to sit at room temperature until it softens.

Prepare your area for cake decorating and gather the following equipment and tools: a cake turntable (optional), masking tape, a 6-inch (15-cm) cake board, two piping bags, a 1M piping tip, a small offset spatula and a pastry scraper (optional).

Carrot Cake Bases

¾ cup (97.5 g) soaked and dehydrated almonds (see Prep Notes on page 20)

1 cup (80 g) medium-shred unsweetened dried coconut

½ cup (56 g) coconut flour

3 tbsp (21 g) ground golden flax (see Prep Notes on page 18)

2 tbsp (16 g) mesquite powder (optional)

1 tbsp (9 g) powdered psyllium (see Prep Notes on page 18)

1 tbsp (8 g) ground cinnamon

¾ tsp ground nutmeg

¼ tsp ground cloves

¼ tsp Himalayan salt

2¾ cups packed (310 g) shredded carrot

¾ cup (180 ml) filtered water

8 large Medjool dates, soaked, pitted and chopped

½ cup (50 g) raw walnuts, soaked for 4 hours and rinsed

¼ cup (60 ml) coconut nectar

¼ cup (37.5 g) raisins, soaked for 20 minutes and drained

1 tbsp (5 g) grated fresh ginger

Secure the cake board to the cake turntable (if using) with a piece of masking tape underneath the cake board. Fill a piping bag with the orange cheesecake frosting and cut off the tip to create a ⅜-inch (1-cm)-diameter hole. Place a dollop of frosting in the center of the board and place one cake base on top, securing it in place. Using the piping bag, create a dam of frosting on the outer edge of the cake base. Place a layer of scattered raisins on the frosting and pipe a layer of frosting on top. Top it off with the second cake base and repeat this process until the third cake base has been secured.

Refill the piping bag with more frosting and create a layer of frosting on the outside of the cake, starting from the bottom in a circular motion, until the entire exterior of the cake is covered. Create a layer of frosting also on top. You should have used the whole batch of frosting. Smooth the frosting vertically from bottom to top, using a small offset spatula.

Using your pastry scraper in a vertical position, gently scrape the sides of the cake while moving your cake turntable (if using) to even out the layer. If you don't have a pastry scraper, feel free to use an offset spatula to smooth the frosting. Be careful not to remove too much frosting. Smooth the top with a small offset spatula and remove excess frosting from the edges. If you're adding the spiced walnut crumble, press it into the bottom of the cake to about 2 inches (5 cm) in height from the bottom, creating a barrier all the way around.

Remove the coconut frosting from the fridge as we will use this on top as a garnish. Fit a Wilton 1M piping tip to a fresh piping bag and fill the piping bag with coconut frosting. Hold the piping bag vertically above the cake and create dollops of frosting around the edge of the cake, squeezing the piping bag with even pressure. Garnish the cake with edible flowers (if using) and some extra spiced walnut crumble (if using). Serve immediately or, without adding the flowers, store in the fridge for three days or in the freezer for up to 1 month.

Assembly
½ cup (75 g) raisins
½ batch Coconut Frosting (page 148)
Edible flowers (optional)

THREE-LAYER TIRAMISU CAKE

Yield: One three-layer 4-inch (10-cm) cake

This is one of those epic recipes you would never believe is raw or vegan. The texture resembles that of a baked cake, and all the flavors are similar to a traditional tiramisu cake, minus the rum. We culture the mascarpone cream to give it that cheeselike flavor. For frosting the cake, you will need cake decorating tools, such as piping bags, an offset spatula, a pastry scraper (optional), a cake board and a cake turntable (optional). Check out the Substitutions List (page 160) for maca powder alternatives.

MASCARPONE CREAM

Open the two probiotics capsules and pour the contents into a blender. Add the cashews, coconut meat and water, and blend until smooth. Transfer the mixture to a glass bowl, cover the top with parchment paper and cover the bowl with cling film or parchment paper and an elastic to seal it. Cover the bowl with an additional tea towel to ensure it's not exposed to light. UV light destroys good bacteria during the fermentation process. Place the bowl in a warm area for 12 hours; don't culture this recipe for too long, as we don't want it to be overpowering.

You can get started on the other components while the mixture is culturing. Once it is done culturing, place it back into the blender along with the agave, lemon juice and melted coconut oil and blend until incorporated. Transfer the mixture to a shallow container and place in the fridge to set for a minimum of 6 hours.

MOCHA FROSTING

In a high-powered blender, blend together the cashews, coconut nectar, coffee, cacao powder, cacao nibs, espresso powder (if using) and vanilla until smooth. Add the melted coconut oil and blend again until combined. The mixture will be thick and will require your tamper.

Transfer the frosting to a shallow container and chill in the fridge for a minimum of 8 hours or overnight, to set. This frosting is very firm and will need a couple of hours at room temperature to soften for piping.

(continued)

Mascarpone Cream

2 capsules dairy-free probiotics

1 cup (140 g) raw cashews, soaked for 2 hours and rinsed

1 cup (160) chopped young coconut meat

½ cup (120 ml) filtered water

2 tbsp (43 ml) light-amber agave

1 tsp fresh lemon juice

¼ cup (60 ml) melted virgin coconut oil

Mocha Frosting

1½ cups (210 g) raw cashews, soaked for 2 hours and rinsed

½ cup (120 ml) coconut nectar

¼ cup + 2 tbsp (90 ml) brewed strong coffee

¼ cup (24 g) cacao powder

3 tbsp (22.5 g) cacao nibs

¼ tsp espresso powder (optional)

12 drops vanilla extract, Medicine Flower brand preferred

½ cup + 2 tbsp (150 ml) melted virgin coconut oil

THREE-LAYER TIRAMISU CAKE
(continued)

"LADYFINGER" CAKE BASES

Blend the coconut in a dry blender to break it down, then transfer to a large bowl. To the bowl, add the almond pulp, powdered coconut sugar, maca powder, psyllium and salt and mix well with your hands until combined, removing all clumps. In a blender, blend together the apples, lemon juice and vanilla into a puree, then add the puree to the bowl and mix with your hands until combined. Last, add the melted cacao butter and mix again.

Line a small cutting board or tray with parchment paper and remove the bottom of three 4-inch (10-cm) springform pans. Place the pans on the lined tray or cutting board with the indent at the top. Fill each pan with the cake batter up to a 1-inch (2.5-cm) depth, smoothing out the top with a back of a spoon. Set the cake bases on the prepared tray and chill in the freezer for a minimum of 3 hours. You want the cake bases frozen when frosting the cake, so the bases don't break apart while frosting.

ASSEMBLY

Remove the mocha frosting from the fridge for a few hours to ensure it's soft enough for piping. This is a firm frosting that holds up really well at room temperature. Prepare your area for cake decorating by gathering the following equipment and tools: a cake turntable (optional), a 6-inch (15-cm) cake board, masking tape, three piping bags, a squeeze bottle or piping bag, a 1M piping tip, a small offset spatula and a pastry scraper (optional).

Secure the cake board to the cake turntable (if using) with a piece of masking tape. Fill a piping bag with the mocha frosting and cut off the tip to create a ⅜-inch (1-cm)-diameter hole. Do the same with the mascarpone cream. Place a dollop of mocha frosting in the center of the board and place one cake base in the center, securing it on top of the frosting. Using the piping bag with the mocha frosting, create a layer on top of the cake base only around the edge. Fill the middle with the mascarpone cream.

Secure a second cake base on top and repeat the process until the third cake base has been placed. Reserve some mascarpone cream for decoration on top. Refill the piping bag with more mocha frosting and create a thick layer of frosting on the outside of the cake bases from top to bottom, starting from the bottom in a circular motion, until the entire exterior of the cake is covered. Create a layer of frosting on top as well. You should have used the whole batch of the mocha frosting. Using a small offset spatula, smooth the frosting vertically from bottom to top.

"Ladyfinger" Cake Bases

1 cup (80 g) medium-shred unsweetened dried coconut

¾ cup (149 g) fresh almond pulp (left over from making Almond Milk; see page 24)

¼ cup (36 g) powdered coconut sugar (see Prep Notes on page 18)

2 tbsp (30 g) maca powder

2 tbsp (18 g) powdered psyllium (see Prep Notes on page 18)

⅛ tsp Himalayan salt

3 cups (375 g) peeled, cored and chopped red apple (about 5 small apples)

2 tbsp (30 ml) fresh lemon juice

12 drops vanilla extract, Medicine Flower brand preferred

2 tbsp (25 g) chopped and melted cacao butter

Using your pastry scraper in a vertical position, gently scrape the sides of the cake while moving your cake turntable (if using) to even out the layer. If you don't have a pastry scraper, feel free to use an offset spatula to smooth the frosting. Be careful not to remove too much frosting. Smooth the top with a small offset spatula and remove excess frosting from the edges. Secure the cacao espresso dust around the bottom of the cake, creating a layer all the way around about 2 inches (5 cm) in height.

Fit a Wilton 1M piping tip to a second piping bag and fill the piping bag with the rest of the mascarpone cream. Hold the piping bag vertically above the cake and create dollops of frosting around the cake, squeezing the piping bag with even pressure. Garnish the top of the mascarpone cream with coffee beans. Transfer the cake to the freezer to cool while you make the dark chocolate ganache.

Once you have the dark chocolate ganache made, transfer it to a squeeze bottle or piping bag. Ensure the cake is cool. Place the cake back on the cake turntable (if using) and create a drip effect around the cake in between the mascarpone cream on its outside edge. The ganache drips should start setting on the cake in different lengths if it's cold enough. Serve immediately or store in the fridge for up to 3 days. This cake freezes well for up to 1 month in the freezer. If stored in the freezer, thaw in the fridge overnight before serving.

Assembly

1 batch Cacao Espresso Dust (page 92)

½ batch Dark Chocolate Ganache (page 153)

Coffee beans

PERFECT PASTRIES AND COOKIES

I would have to say that dehydrated pastry is my specialty. Dehydrating is my favorite technique in raw cuisine, as a dehydrator creates a variety of textures, and it's a lot of fun to experiment with. I'm like a mad scientist in the kitchen when it comes to dehydrating. In this chapter, you'll get to experience working with raw dough and see it's not that much different than conventional dough. We use raw flours and a rolling pin to create and shape the dough for the cookies.

The first recipe you will want to check out is the Mocha Donuts with Espresso Glaze (page 92). Most raw donut recipes are made with a base of nuts and dates, which in my opinion, is just a glorified energy bite; why not make something closer to the real thing? I use raw flours, psyllium and other ingredients to create a texture that would have you second-guessing whether they have been baked or not.

This chapter also includes dehydrated cookies, such as ones reminiscent of your childhood cookie sandwiches with raw jam. If you love citrus desserts, you will love the Lemon Poppy Seed Coconut Shortbread Cookies (page 86); they are so light and refreshing. I know you'll really enjoy working with your dehydrator on these recipes and seeing all the possibilities it creates.

LEMON POPPY SEED COCONUT SHORTBREAD COOKIES

If you want a refreshing snack, these lemony, nut-free cookies hit the spot. They are dehydrated to create a crunchy texture, and the luscious lemon cream filling is the perfect addition. For this recipe, make sure to have some Coconut Milk (page 27) and coconut pulp prepared ahead of time. Coconut pulp is one of my favorite ingredients in cookies and cakes. It adds a light, fluffy texture. This recipe uses young coconut meat, but check out the Substitutions List (page 160) for other options.

Yield: 14 cookies
Nut-free

LEMON COCONUT CREAM FILLING

In a high-speed blender, blend together the young coconut meat, lemon juice, coconut milk, powdered xylitol, sunflower lecithin, turmeric, salt and vanilla until smooth. Add the melted coconut oil and blend again until combined. Transfer the mixture to a shallow container and chill in the fridge for a minimum of 8 hours or overnight, until firm.

(continued)

Lemon Coconut Cream Filling

1 cup (160 g) chopped young coconut meat

¼ cup (60 ml) fresh lemon juice

¼ cup (60 ml) Coconut Milk (page 27)

3 tbsp (36 g) powdered xylitol (see Prep Notes on page 18)

1½ tsp (4 scant g) sunflower lecithin powder

¼ tsp ground turmeric

⅛ tsp Himalayan salt

3 drops vanilla extract, Medicine Flower brand preferred

¼ cup (60 ml) melted virgin coconut oil

LEMON POPPY SEED COCONUT SHORTBREAD COOKIES
(continued)

LEMON SHORTBREAD COOKIES

In a food processor, process the coconut, coconut flour, ground flax and psyllium until the coconut is broken down and resembles coarse flour. Add the coconut pulp, coconut milk, softened coconut butter, agave, lemon juice and zest and vanilla, and process until the batter is well combined. Last, add the poppy seeds and pulse until evenly incorporated.

The batter will not form a ball and will look crumbly, but it will stick together if you squeeze it together in your hands. Secure a piece of parchment paper or a reusable dehydrator sheet to the countertop with masking tape. Place the cookie dough on top of the paper and place another piece of parchment paper or a reusable dehydrator sheet on top. Keep a small bowl of water close by as the cookie dough will dry up fast. If it dries out while you're working with it, add a little of the water and work it into the dough with your hands.

Flatten the dough ball with your hands and use a rolling pin to roll the cookie dough to about ¼ inch (6 mm) thick. Use a small round cookie cutter to form the cookies and transfer them carefully to a mesh-lined dehydrator tray, using a small offset spatula by scooping them up from underneath. Repeat the process until you have used all the cookie dough. You should have 28 cookie disks.

Dehydrate at 115°F (46°C) for 4½ hours, or until the cookies are dried on the outside but still soft on the inside. Allow the cookies to cool before assembling.

ASSEMBLY

Remove the lemon cream filling from the fridge and check the consistency for piping. If it's too soft, chill in the freezer for 10 to 20 minutes, then stir the frosting around, whipping it up. If the cream filling is too firm, allow it to sit at room temperature until it softens.

Fit a Wilton 1M piping tip to a piping bag and fill the piping bag with the lemon cream filling. Place a dollop of frosting in the middle of a cookie and place another cookie on top. Repeat this process until you've assembled all 14 cookies. Serve immediately or store in the fridge for up to 3 days or in the freezer for up to 1 month.

Lemon Shortbread Cookies

⅓ cup (25 g) medium-shred unsweetened dried coconut

1½ tbsp (10.5 g) coconut flour

1 tbsp (7 g) ground golden flax (see Prep Notes on page 18)

1½ tsp (4.5 g) powdered psyllium (see Prep Notes on page 18)

½ cup (70 g) coconut pulp (left over from making Coconut Milk; see page 27)

2 tbsp (30 ml) Coconut Milk (page 27)

2 tbsp (30 g) softened Coconut Butter (page 31)

2 tbsp (43 ml) light-amber agave

1 tbsp (15 ml) fresh lemon juice

1 tsp lemon zest

3 drops vanilla extract, Medicine Flower brand preferred

1½ tsp (4 g) poppy seeds

MATCHA RASPBERRY LINZER COOKIES

Linzer cookies are popular during the holidays, probably because they are as delicious as they are fun to create. You will need linzer cookie cutters for this recipe, which are quite easy to source. Have fun with all the different designs offered. We use matcha powder in this recipe to switch up the traditional version and work with the season's festive colors.

Yield: 12 cookies

DEHYDRATED RASPBERRY JAM

In a bowl, combine the thawed raspberries, coconut nectar and salt and mash with a whisk until the raspberries are broken down. Do not blend this mixture, or too much liquid will be released. Place the bowl on a lower dehydrator tray and dehydrate at 115°F (46°C) for 18 to 24 hours, or until reduced and thick. Transfer the jam to a sealed container and place in the fridge for a few hours to thicken up further. Once cooled, it will resemble a thick, chunky jam.

MATCHA COOKIES

In a food processor, process the coconut flour, almonds, activated oat flour, ground flax, lucuma powder and matcha powder together until the mixture resembles coarse flour. Add the water, agave, sesame oil, lemon zest and vanilla, and process again until the batter forms a dough ball.

Secure a piece of parchment paper or a reusable dehydrator sheet to the countertop with masking tape. Place the cookie dough on top of the paper and place another piece of parchment paper or reusable dehydrator sheet on top. Press the dough ball down firmly before using a rolling pin to smooth it out. Roll out the dough to about ¼ inch (6 mm) thick, using a rolling pin.

Use the linzer cookie cutters as per the manufacturer's instructions to cut cookies from the rolled-out dough. You will need to form one solid cookie base and one top, which will have a design cut out of the center. These will form one cookie. Carefully transfer the base and top to a mesh-lined dehydrator tray, using an offset spatula and lifting them up from underneath. Repeat the process until you have used all the dough. (You should have 12 bases and 12 cutout tops.) Dehydrate at 115°F (46°C) for 12 hours, or until the cookies are dried.

(continued)

Dehydrated Raspberry Jam

2 cups (284 g) frozen raspberries, thawed (measured before thawing)

⅓ cup (80 ml) coconut nectar

⅛ tsp Himalayan salt

Matcha Cookies

½ cup + 1 tbsp (63 g) coconut flour

½ cup (65 g) soaked and dehydrated almonds (see Prep Notes on page 20)

¼ cup (33 g) Activated Oat Flour (page 28)

1 tbsp (7 g) ground golden flax (see Prep Notes on page 18)

1 tbsp (7.5 g) lucuma powder

2 tsp (4 g) matcha powder

¼ cup + 2 tbsp (90 ml) water

2 tbsp (43 ml) light-amber agave

2 tbsp (30 ml) cold-pressed sesame oil

½ tsp lemon zest

6 drops vanilla extract, Medicine Flower brand preferred

MATCHA RASPBERRY
LINZER COOKIES (continued)

ASSEMBLY

Fill a piping bag with the raspberry jam and cut off the tip of the piping bag to create a hole ⅜ inch (1 cm) in diameter. Squeeze jam from the piping bag onto the middle of a cookie base and place a cutout cookie on top. Be careful not to add too much jam, to prevent it from leaking out over the edges. Repeat this process until you have filled and sandwiched all 12 complete linzer cookies. Add some powdered xylitol to a small fine-mesh strainer and dust the top of the cookies with the powdered xylitol for decoration.

Serve immediately or store in the fridge for up to 3 days. Once assembled, the cookies do not freeze well because the jam does not freeze. The cookie bases freeze well separately.

PRO TIP: If you want to make these ahead of time, store the cookies and jam separately in the fridge and assemble them before serving. The cookies will get a little soggy after a few days if placed assembled in the fridge. These do not freeze well assembled, as the raspberry jam does not freeze.

Assembly

Powdered xylitol (see Prep Notes on page 18)

MOCHA DONUTS WITH ESPRESSO GLAZE

I do not drink coffee, but coffee and chocolate is my all-time favorite flavor combo in desserts. Not only are these raw donuts delicious, but they are unique because they are prepared in a dehydrator. We use raw flours to create a raw pastry texture and sneak in a vegetable to lighten up the batter. Mesquite powder is optional, but definitely use it in this recipe if you can source it because it adds a caramel flavor. Decorating these with the different garnishes is a lot of fun.

Yield: 8 to 10 donuts

CACAO ESPRESSO DUST

In a coffee grinder, spice grinder or blender, coarsely grind the whole coffee beans. In a food processor, process the ground coffee beans, walnuts, cacao powder, powdered coconut sugar, coconut nectar, salt and vanilla together into a crumble.

Spread the mixture on a lined dehydrator tray and dehydrate at 115°F (46°C) for 18 to 24 hours, or until dried, flipping the batch halfway through. Once it is done in the dehydrator, allow it to cool and process again in the food processor to form a crumble. Store in the freezer until ready to use. This mixture will keep in the freezer for months.

MOCHA DONUTS

In a food processor, process the almonds, cacao powder, coconut flour, powdered coconut sugar, activated oat flour, mesquite powder (if using), psyllium, espresso powder (if using) and salt together until the mixture resembles coarse flour.

(continued)

Cacao Espresso Dust

½ cup (40 g) organic whole coffee beans

½ cup (50 g) raw walnuts, soaked for 4 hours and rinsed

¼ cup (24 g) cacao powder

¼ cup (36 g) powdered coconut sugar (see Prep Notes on page 18)

2 tbsp (30 ml) coconut nectar

⅛ tsp Himalayan salt

6 drops vanilla extract, Medicine Flower brand preferred

Mocha Donuts

¾ cup (97.5 g) soaked and dehydrated almonds (see Prep Notes on page 20)

¾ cup (72 g) cacao powder

½ cup (56 g) coconut flour

½ cup (72 g) powdered coconut sugar (see Prep Notes on page 18)

¼ cup (33 g) Activated Oat Flour (page 28)

2 tbsp (16 g) mesquite powder (optional)

2 tbsp (18 g) powdered psyllium (see Prep Notes on page 18)

¼ tsp espresso powder (optional)

⅛ tsp Himalayan salt

(continued)

MOCHA DONUTS WITH
ESPRESSO GLAZE (continued)

Add the zucchini, coconut nectar, cacao nibs, sesame oil, vanilla and coffee extract, and process until thoroughly combined. The mixture will be very moist—this is normal. After a little while, the coconut flour and psyllium will absorb a lot of the moisture and the batter will thicken up.

Transfer the batter to a silicone donut mold by pressing the dough firmly into each donut cavity and scraping the excess dough off the top. Place the silicone mold on a dehydrator tray and dehydrate at 115°F (46°C) for 1½ hours. Remove the donuts from the silicone mold and transfer them to a mesh dehydrator tray. Continue to dehydrate for another 5½ to 7 hours, or until they are dried on the outside but still moist inside.

Transfer the donuts to a container and place them in the fridge to cool while you make the espresso glaze. The donuts need to be cooled for the glaze to set on them.

ESPRESSO GLAZE
In a blender, blend together the cashews, coffee, powdered coconut sugar, melted cacao butter, coconut nectar, lemon juice, salt, vanilla and coffee extract until smooth. If the mixture starts to curdle or create texture, keep blending until it is smooth. The heat produced by the blender will help. You may need to use your tamper.

Once the donuts are cooled, transfer the glaze to a small bowl and prepare your area for glazing and decorating.

ASSEMBLY
Melt or make the enrobing dark chocolate and transfer the melted chocolate to a squeeze bottle or piping bag for decorating. Place some of the cacao espresso dust in a small bowl and line a tray or cutting board with parchment paper. Begin to glaze the donuts, one at a time, by dipping one, upside down, into the bowl of espresso glaze, then lift the donut out of the bowl and allow the excess glaze to drip off. Repeat this process so the donut is double glazed.

Place the donut, right side up, on the prepared surface. Immediately garnish with some cacao espresso dust as the glaze will start setting quickly. Repeat this process and then drizzle the top with the melted enrobing dark chocolate. If using a piping bag, cut off the tip to create a small hole.

Repeat until all the donuts are glazed, dusted and garnished. Serve immediately or allow them to set in the fridge. Store the donuts in the fridge for up to 1 week or in the freezer for 1 month.

1 cup (120 g) peeled and chopped zucchini

½ cup (120 ml) coconut nectar

¼ cup + 2 tbsp (45 g) cacao nibs

2 tbsp (30 ml) cold-pressed sesame oil

15 drops vanilla extract, Medicine Flower brand preferred

8 drops coffee extract, Medicine Flower brand preferred

Espresso Glaze

¾ cup (105 g) raw cashews, soaked for 2 hours and rinsed

¼ cup (60 ml) warm brewed organic coffee

¼ cup (36 g) powdered coconut sugar (see Prep Notes on page 18)

¼ cup (50 g) chopped and melted cacao butter

2 tbsp (30 ml) coconut nectar

1.5 tsp (8 ml) fresh lemon juice

⅛ tsp Himalayan salt

6 drops vanilla extract, Medicine Flower brand preferred

2 drops coffee extract, Medicine Flower brand preferred

Assembly

½ batch Enrobing Dark Chocolate (page 156)

ALMOND FIG AND CARDAMOM COOKIE SANDWICHES

This recipe uses fresh almond pulp to create these delicious, moist, dehydrated cookies. These are filled with a dehydrated fig jam and topped with chai-spiced icing, with all the warm flavors of fall. If you are unable to source golden figs, check out the Substitutions List (page 160) for other options.

Yield: 10 cookie sandwiches

ALMOND COOKIES

In a blender, blend the coconut until broken down (do not overblend, or you will end up making coconut butter), then transfer to a large bowl. Rinse the blender and blend the chopped apples and dates to make a puree. Transfer the puree to the bowl of coconut.

To the same bowl, add the almond pulp, ground flax, coconut flour, sesame oil, mesquite powder, psyllium and orange zest, and mix the batter well with your hands, removing all clumps. Secure a piece of parchment paper or a reusable dehydrator sheet to the countertop with masking tape. Place the cookie dough on top of the paper and place another piece of parchment paper or reusable dehydrator sheet on top of the cookie dough.

Press the dough ball down firmly and, using a rolling pin, roll out the dough to about ½ inch (1.3 cm) thick. Use a 2.5-inch (6.5-cm) round cookie cutter to form cookies and transfer the cookies, using a small offset spatula, onto a mesh-lined dehydrator tray. Repeat the process until you have used all the dough. You should have 20 cookie disks. Dehydrate the cookies at 115°F (46°C) for 12 hours, or until dried.

(continued)

Almond Cookies

1 cup (80 g) medium-shred unsweetened dried coconut

2 cups (250 g) unpeeled, cored and chopped red apple (about 2 apples)

¾ cup (134 g) Medjool dates, soaked for 30 minutes and pitted (about 7 to 8 dates)

¾ cup (149 g) almond pulp (left over from making Almond Milk; see page 24)

¼ cup (28 g) ground golden flax (see Prep Notes on page 18)

2 tbsp (14 g) coconut flour

2 tbsp (30 ml) cold-pressed sesame oil

1 tbsp (8 g) mesquite powder

1 tbsp (9 g) powdered psyllium (see Prep Notes on page 18)

2 tsp (4 g) orange zest

ALMOND FIG AND CARDAMOM COOKIE SANDWICHES
(continued)

FIG AND CARDAMOM JAM

In a food processor, process the figs, raisins, almond milk, coconut nectar, ginger, cinnamon, cardamom and salt together until they form a paste. Transfer to a bowl, place the bowl on a lower dehydrator tray and dehydrate the jam at 115°F (46°C) for 2 hours, or until the jam is reduced and thick. Transfer the jam to the fridge to cool.

CHAI-SPICED ICING

Only make this when you're ready to garnish the cookie sandwiches. In a high-powered blender, blend together the cashews, water, coconut nectar, cinnamon, cardamom, ginger, vanilla and pepper until smooth. Transfer the mixture to a squeeze bottle for decorating.

ASSEMBLY

Place a dollop of jam (about 1 teaspoon) on top of one cookie and place another cookie on top. Repeat this process until you have assembled all 10 cookies. Drizzle some of the chai-spiced icing on top.

Serve immediately or store the components separately in the fridge. The cookie bases freeze well. Once they are thawed, they are best warmed in the dehydrator. The fig jam does not freeze well, but will keep in the fridge for up to 5 days.

Fig and Cardamom Jam

1 cup (155 g) packed dried golden figs, soaked for 30 minutes in warm water and drained

½ cup (75 g) raisins, soaked for 30 minutes in warm water

¼ cup (60 ml) Almond Milk (page 24)

2 tbsp (30 ml) coconut nectar

1 tsp grated fresh ginger

1 tsp ground cinnamon

¼ tsp ground cardamom

⅛ tsp Himalayan salt

Chai-Spiced Icing

¾ cup (105 g) raw cashews, soaked for 2 hours and rinsed

¼ cup (60 ml) water

¼ cup (60 ml) coconut nectar

¼ tsp ground cinnamon

¼ tsp ground cardamom

¼ tsp ground ginger

6 drops vanilla extract, Medicine Flower brand preferred

Pinch of freshly ground black pepper

MANGO BERRY CRÊPES WITH COCONUT CREAM

Crêpes are a fun dish to make and perfect for breakfast, brunch or dessert. These crêpes are dehydrated and made without coconut meat, using mango and zucchini instead. Flax and psyllium are essential in this recipe as they act as a binder to add flexibility to the crêpes.

Yield: 9 crêpes

MANGO CRÊPES

In a blender, blend together the thawed mango, zucchini, agave, water, lime juice, lucuma powder (if using) and vanilla until smooth. Add the ground flax and psyllium, and blend until combined. The batter will start thickening quickly with the flax and psyllium added; you may need your tamper for blending.

Spread the crêpe batter on a square, lined dehydrator tray, using an offset spatula to spread it to the outer edges, covering the tray. The batter will fit on one 14 x 14-inch (35.5 x 35.5-cm) tray, with a little left over to spread on another lined dehydrator tray. The batter should be thin and as even as you can spread it. If the batter is difficult to spread, dip your offset spatula in water before each use.

Dehydrate at 105°F (40.5°C) on the liner for 5 hours. Remove the tray, flip the crêpes onto a mesh-lined dehydrator tray and continue to dehydrate for another 30 to 45 minutes. The key to keeping the crêpes flexible while dehydrating is to leave them on the liner until they are almost completely dried. Once you flip them, you will see pockets of areas that are not fully dried; flipping them onto the mesh allows those areas to dry. If the edges start drying out, spread a little water on the outside edges and put them back into the dehydrator. Once they are dried, cut the crêpes into 4-inch (10-cm) squares and store them in the fridge until ready to use.

ASSEMBLY

Place a crêpe on a tray or cutting board and fill a piping bag with the vanilla bean coconut whip. Create a zigzag of the coconut whip from one corner to the opposite corner and place the strawberries on top. Wrap the crêpe and seal it by spreading a little water on the top layer corner. Drizzle the crêpes with chocolate sauce and top with fresh blackberries and microgreens or fresh mint when serving. Serve immediately as the crêpes will soften once assembled. Extra crêpes will keep in the fridge for 1 week or in the freezer for up to 1 month.

Mango Crêpes

1 cup (150 g) frozen mango, thawed (measured before thawing)

1 cup (120 g) peeled and chopped zucchini

2 tbsp (43 ml) light-amber agave

¼ cup + 2 tbsp (90 ml) filtered water

1 tbsp (15 ml) fresh lime juice

1 tbsp (7.5 g) lucuma powder (optional, for extra flavor boost)

4 drops vanilla extract, Medicine Flower brand preferred

¼ cup (28 g) ground golden flax (see Prep Notes on page 18)

1 tbsp (9 g) powdered psyllium (see Prep Notes on page 18)

Assembly

1 batch Vanilla Bean Coconut Whip (page 157)

½ cup (83 g) small-diced strawberries, tops removed

½ batch Chocolate Sauce (page 154)

4 fresh blackberries, cut in half

Microgreens or fresh mint

PRO TIP: Do not increase the temperature past 105°F (40.5°C). This is a suitable temperature for crêpes and wraps to ensure they stay flexible and dehydrate evenly.

HEALTHIER PIES
AND TARTS

This chapter has a pie or tart for every palate and occasion. Each one is decorated uniquely, with a variation of piping techniques using an assortment of piping tips. It's a good idea to practice your piping skills first on a piece of parchment paper before piping onto the finished product.

You'll enjoy the array of crusts in this chapter and discover that you don't always have to rely on dates to create raw crusts. These crusts are date-free, crunchy, delicious and easy to remove from the tart pans without lining them.

Have you ever had a raw pecan pie? Once you try Pecan Pie with Rosemary and Orange (page 107), I can tell you that it will be the only raw pecan pie recipe you'll ever need. Pecan pie was one of my favorite desserts while growing up, so creating this raw version was nostalgic for me. My favorite tart recipe in this chapter is probably the Chocolate Hazelnut Praline Tarts (page 105); as you know by now, chocolate is my number one choice!

CHOCOLATE MINT CREAM TARTS

These tarts are simple yet elegant. Chocolate and mint is one of my favorite flavor combinations. We use food-grade peppermint essential oil to achieve a lovely mint flavor, but you can use mint extract instead. Moringa powder is used as a natural superfood color to create a pastel-green color in the mint cream filling.

Yield: Three 4-inch (10-cm) tarts

CACAO COCONUT CRUST

In a food processor, process the almonds, coconut, cacao powder and powdered coconut sugar together until the mixture resembles coarse flour. Add the melted cacao butter, coconut nectar and vanilla, and process again until the mixture starts sticking together. Do not overprocess the mixture, or you will start to release too many oils from the almonds and coconut.

Using your fingers, divide the crust mixture equally among three 4-inch (10-cm) round tart pans with a removable bottom and use a small spoon to even out the bottom of each crust. Set them aside at room temperature while you make the filling.

MINT CREAM

In a blender, blend together the cashews, almond milk, coconut nectar, sunflower lecithin (if using), moringa powder, peppermint essential oil and vanilla until smooth. Add the melted cacao butter and blend again until well combined. Pour the mint cream into each tart pan and gently pat the tart pans on the counter to remove any air bubbles.

ASSEMBLY

Make or melt the enrobing dark chocolate and transfer the melted chocolate to a squeeze bottle or piping bag for decorating. If using a piping bag, cut a small hole on the end of the tip. Create horizontal lines a scant ¼ inch (6 mm) apart on top of the mint filling. Using a toothpick, run the toothpick through the horizontal lines vertically, going in opposite directions, to create a beautiful design.

Chill the tarts in the freezer for a minimum of 4 hours. Thaw at room temperature for 30 minutes, slice and serve. Store in the fridge for 5 days or in the freezer for up to 1 month.

PRO TIP: The tart pans do not need to be lined since we are not using any sticky ingredients, such as dried fruit. Once the crust is set, it will pop right out of the mold.

Cacao Coconut Crust

1 cup (130 g) soaked and dehydrated almonds (see Prep Notes on page 20)

1 cup (80 g) medium-shred unsweetened dried coconut

¼ cup + 2 tbsp (36 g) cacao powder

2 tbsp (18 g) powdered coconut sugar (see Prep Notes on page 18)

3 tbsp (37.5 g) chopped and melted cacao butter

2 tbsp (30 ml) coconut nectar

10 drops vanilla extract, Medicine Flower brand preferred

Mint Cream

1 cup (140 g) raw cashews, soaked for 2 hours and rinsed

½ cup (120 ml) Almond Milk (page 24)

¼ cup (60 ml) coconut nectar

1½ tsp (scant 4 ml) sunflower lecithin powder (optional)

1 tbsp (6 g) moringa powder (for color and nutrition boost)

10 drops food-grade peppermint essential oil

6 drops vanilla extract, Medicine Flower brand preferred

2 tbsp (25 g) chopped and melted cacao butter

Assembly

½ batch Enrobing Dark Chocolate (page 156)

CHOCOLATE HAZELNUT PRALINE TARTS

Yield: Three 4-inch (10-cm) tarts

This is a chocolate lover's dream with an elegant finish! Hazelnut and chocolate is a very popular flavor combination and this recipe knocks it out of the park. Make sure to have some Double Chocolate Frosting (page 150) prepared for this recipe; we also do a really fun piping technique on this one! It's important to have all the ingredients for the hazelnut chocolate filling at room temperature; if they are cold, once you add the cacao butter, the mixture will seize and start setting, causing the filling to be challenging to work with. Chocolate requires patience. You can always refer to my section on Troubleshooting Chocolate (page 21) for more insight.

HAZELNUT PRALINE

In a food processor, process the hazelnuts, cacao nibs, coconut nectar and vanilla together until the mixture forms a large crumble. Spread the mixture on a lined dehydrator tray and dehydrate at 115°F (46°C) for 24 hours. The mixture will feel sticky until cool and will crisp up in the freezer. Chill the mixture in the freezer until ready to use.

HAZELNUT CHOCOLATE CRUST

In a food processor, process the hazelnuts, activated oat flour, cacao powder and powdered coconut sugar together until the mixture resembles coarse flour. Add the melted cacao butter, coconut nectar and vanilla, and process the mixture until the batter starts sticking together.

Using your fingers, divide the crust mixture equally among three 4-inch (10-cm) round tart pans with a removable bottom and use a small spoon to even out the bottom of each crust. Set them aside at room temperature while you make the filling.

(continued)

Hazelnut Praline

1 cup (135 g) raw hazelnuts, soaked for 2 hours and rinsed

¼ cup (30 g) cacao nibs

¼ cup (60 ml) coconut nectar

6 drops vanilla extract, Medicine Flower brand preferred

Hazelnut Chocolate Crust

1 cup (135 g) raw hazelnuts

¾ cup (98 g) Activated Oat Flour (page 28)

¼ cup (24 g) cacao powder

2 tbsp (18 g) powdered coconut sugar (see Prep Notes on page 18)

3 tbsp (37.5 g) chopped and melted cacao butter

2 tbsp (30 ml) coconut nectar

10 drops vanilla extract, Medicine Flower brand preferred

HAZELNUT CHOCOLATE FILLING

In a blender, blend together the hazelnut milk, coconut nectar, cacao powder, mesquite powder, hazelnut butter, vanilla and salt until smooth. While the blender is running on low speed, slowly add the melted cacao paste and melted cacao butter until incorporated. The mixture will be thick but should still be pourable.

Fill each tart crust with the filling, using a small offset spatula to smooth out the top. Set the tarts in the freezer or the fridge for a couple of hours. The filling sets quickly. While you're waiting for the filling to set, remove the double chocolate frosting from the fridge to allow it to soften at room temperature for piping.

ASSEMBLY

Once the double chocolate frosting is softened enough for piping, remove the tarts from the fridge or freezer and remove them from their pans. Fit an Ateco 882 piping tip to a piping bag and fill the piping bag with the double chocolate frosting. Holding the piping bag in a horizontal position with the open end of the tip facing up on top of a tart, start creating a ribbon, zigzagging horizontally on the tart until the entire top is covered.

Remove the hazelnut praline from the freezer. If the praline is stuck together, blitz it in a food processor for a few seconds until it is broken up. Garnish the top of the frosting with the hazelnut praline. Serve immediately or store the tarts in the fridge for up to 5 days. These tarts also freeze well for up to 1 month.

Hazelnut Chocolate Filling

½ cup (120 ml) Hazelnut Milk (page 25), at room temperature

⅓ cup (80 ml) coconut nectar

2 tbsp (12 g) cacao powder

2 tbsp (16 g) mesquite powder

1 tbsp (16 g) hazelnut or almond butter

6 drops vanilla extract, Medicine Flower brand preferred

⅛ tsp Himalayan salt

½ cup (100 g) chopped and melted cacao paste

40 g chopped cacao butter, melted

Assembly

1 batch Double Chocolate Frosting (page 150)

PECAN PIE WITH ROSEMARY AND ORANGE

I've never had a raw pecan pie I enjoyed until I came up with this one; you will love it! We use Coconut Butter (page 31) in the filling to replicate a buttery, creamy taste. The Himalayan salt in the filling is very important to balance the sweetness; make sure not to omit it.

Yield: Two 4-inch (10-cm) pies

CANDIED PECANS

In a bowl, mix together the soaked pecans, coconut sugar and salt until well combined. Spread on a lined dehydrator tray and dehydrate at 115°F (46°C) for 18 to 24 hours, or until completely dry. Transfer to the freezer to crisp up before use.

ROSEMARY PIECRUST

In a food processor, process the almonds, activated oat flour, mesquite powder (if using), rosemary, cinnamon and salt together until the mixture resembles coarse flour. Add the melted coconut oil and coconut nectar, and process the mixture again until the batter sticks together.

Using your fingers, divide the crust mixture equally between two 4-inch (10-cm) round tart pans with a removable bottom and use a small spoon to even out the bottom of the crust. Set them aside at room temperature while you make the filling.

(continued)

Candied Pecans

1½ cups (150 g) raw pecans, soaked for 4 hours and rinsed

¼ cup (40 g) coconut sugar

Pinch of Himalayan salt

Rosemary Piecrust

1 cup (130 g) soaked and dehydrated almonds (see Prep Notes on page 20)

½ cup (65 g) Activated Oat Flour (page 28)

1 tbsp (8 g) mesquite powder (optional)

1 tsp minced fresh rosemary leaves

½ tsp ground cinnamon

Pinch of Himalayan salt

2 tbsp (30 ml) melted virgin coconut oil

1 tbsp (15 ml) coconut nectar

PECAN PIE WITH ROSEMARY
AND ORANGE (continued)

"BUTTER" PECAN FILLING

In a high-speed blender, blend together the raisins, coconut butter, pecan milk, coconut nectar, orange zest, salt, cinnamon and vanilla until smooth. The mixture should resemble a date paste. Transfer the mixture to a bowl, add the chopped candied pecans and mix until combined.

ASSEMBLY

Fill the tart crusts to the top with the butter pecan filling. Add some whole candied pecans on top in a circular direction as a decoration. Chill the pies in the freezer for 3 to 4 hours, and once they are set, remove the pies from the tart pans. Top with vanilla bean ice cream and serve immediately. The pies will keep in the fridge for up to 5 days or in the freezer for 1 month.

"Butter" Pecan Filling

¾ cup (110 g) raisins, soaked for 30 minutes in warm water and drained

¼ cup (60 g) softened Coconut Butter (page 31)

¼ cup + 2 tbsp (90 ml) Pecan Milk (page 26)

2 tbsp (30 ml) coconut nectar

½ tsp orange zest

¼ tsp Himalayan salt

½ tsp ground cinnamon

3 drops vanilla extract, Medicine Flower brand preferred

½ cup (70 g) chopped Candied Pecans

Assembly

18 whole Candied Pecans

½ batch Vanilla Bean Ice Cream (page 120)

RASPBERRY BEET MOUSSE AND CAROB TARTS

Carob powder looks like cacao but is less bitter and sweeter. We use carob powder in the crust, but you can use cacao powder instead. You will find this tart quite refreshing and beautiful once decorated.

Yield: Three 4-inch (10-cm) tarts

CAROB ALMOND CRUST

In a food processor, process the almonds, activated oat flour, carob powder and powdered coconut sugar together until the mixture resembles coarse flour. Add the coconut nectar, vanilla, melted cacao butter and salt, and process again until the mixture starts sticking together. Do not overprocess the mixture, or you will start to release too many oils from the almonds.

Using your fingers, divide the crust mixture among three 4-inch (10-cm) rectangular tart pans with a removable bottom and use a small spoon to even the bottom of each crust. Set them aside at room temperature while you make the filling.

RASPBERRY BEET MOUSSE

Juice the raspberries and beets per your juicer's instructions. If you do not have a juicer, in a high-speed blender, blend the raspberries and beets with ¼ cup (60 ml) of water and strain through a nut milk bag. This mixture should make 1 cup (240 ml) of raspberry beet juice, which you will use for the filling. If necessary, add filtered water to top it off to an even cup (240 ml).

In a blender, combine the raspberry beet juice, the cashews, coconut nectar, sunflower lecithin and orange zest, and blend until smooth. Lastly, add the melted cacao butter and blend on low speed until well combined. Pour the filling into the tart crusts, taking care to not overfill the tarts. Chill the tarts in the freezer for 6 hours.

ASSEMBLY

Remove the tarts from the freezer and carefully remove them from their pans, removing the bottom of the pan from the bottom of each crust. Decorate and garnish with fresh sliced raspberries, blackberries and mint. Store extra tarts in the fridge with fresh garnishes for up to 3 days or in the freezer for up to 1 month without the fresh garnishes.

Carob Almond Crust

1 cup (130 g) soaked and dehydrated almonds (see Prep Notes on page 20)

¼ cup (33 g) Activated Oat Flour (page 28)

¼ cup (24 g) raw or roasted carob powder

2 tbsp (18 g) powdered coconut sugar (see Prep Notes on page 18)

2 tbsp (30 ml) coconut nectar

3 drops vanilla extract, Medicine Flower brand preferred

2 tbsp (25 g) chopped and melted cacao butter

⅛ tsp Himalayan salt

Raspberry Beet Mousse

1 cup (142 g) frozen raspberries, thawed (measured before thawing)

1 cup (165 g) peeled and chopped beets

½ cup (70 g) raw cashews, soaked for 2 hours and rinsed

¼ cup (60 ml) coconut nectar

1½ tsp (scant 4 g) sunflower lecithin powder

1 tsp packed orange zest

85 g chopped cacao butter, melted

Assembly

Fresh raspberries, sliced in half

Fresh blackberries, sliced in half

Fresh mint leaves

AVOCADO KEY LIME PIES WITH COCONUT CREAM

If you're a fan of citrus desserts or traditional Key lime pie, you will love this raw vegan version. These pies are light, refreshing and look stunning. Make sure to have a batch of Coconut Frosting (page 148) prepared for this recipe. These pies will be sure to impress your friends and family.

Yield: Two 4-inch (10-cm) pies

ALMOND COCONUT CRUST

In a food processor, process the almonds, coconut, coconut flour, coconut sugar and salt together until the mixture resembles coarse flour. Add the lime zest and melted coconut oil, and process the mixture again until the batter starts sticking together.

Using your fingers, divide the crust mixture equally between two 4-inch (10-cm) round tart pans with a removable bottom and use a small spoon to even out the bottom of the crust. Set them aside at room temperature while you make the filling.

AVOCADO LIME FILLING

In a high-speed blender, blend together the avocado, lime juice, coconut cream, agave, lime zest, sunflower lecithin, vanilla and salt until smooth. Add the melted coconut oil and blend again for a few seconds until combined. Pour the filling into each tart pan (you will have left over filling; see next paragraph), and pat the tart pans on the counter to even out the filling. If the filling is thick, use an offset spatula to spread it out.

Place the leftover Key lime pie filling in a bowl, cover and chill it in the fridge to enjoy as a pudding. Chill the pies in the freezer for a minimum of 4 hours or overnight.

(continued)

Almond Coconut Crust

1 cup (130 g) soaked and dehydrated almonds (see Prep Notes on page 20)

⅓ cup (25 g) medium-shred unsweetened dried coconut

¼ cup (28 g) coconut flour

3 tbsp (30 g) coconut sugar

⅛ tsp Himalayan salt

1 tsp lime zest

2 tbsp (30 ml) melted virgin coconut oil

Avocado Lime Filling

½ cup (75 g) peeled, pitted and cubed ripe avocado

¼ cup (60 ml) fresh lime juice

¼ cup (60 ml) Coconut Cream (page 27)

3 tbsp (64 g) light-amber agave

1½ tbsp (3 g) lime zest

1 tsp sunflower lecithin powder

6 drops vanilla extract, Medicine Flower brand preferred

⅛ tsp Himalayan salt

¼ cup (60 ml) melted virgin coconut oil

AVOCADO KEY LIME PIES WITH COCONUT CREAM (continued)

ASSEMBLY

Remove the pies from the freezer and the coconut frosting from the fridge. If the coconut frosting is quite firm, allow it to sit at room temperature until it's soft enough for piping. If it is too soft, chill in the freezer for 10 to 20 minutes to firm up, then whip with a spoon. Remove the pies from the tart pans before garnishing. If the tart pan bottom is difficult to remove, use a butter knife or offset spatula to remove it from the crust.

Fit an Ateco 867 piping tip to a piping bag and fill the piping bag with coconut frosting. Above each pie, hold the piping bag vertically and pipe dollops around the top of the pie in a circular motion, starting from the outside edge, until the entire pie is covered. Using a citrus zester, such as a Microplane, garnish the top of each pie with lime zest. Serve immediately or store the pies in the fridge for up to 3 days or in the freezer for up to 1 month.

Assembly

½ batch Coconut Frosting (page 148)

Zest of 1 lime

BANANA CREAM PIE WITH GINGERBREAD CRUST

This recipe is very nostalgic, taking me back in time to Christmas dinner as a child enjoying all the Christmas desserts at the table. The gingerbread crust plus banana cream is the perfect flavor pairing. This recipe uses young coconut meat, but you can replace it with cashews instead; refer to the Substitutions List (page 160). Agar Paste (page 31) is used in the coconut cream whipped topping and banana cream filling to lighten them up and provide an airy texture.

Yield: Two 4-inch (10-cm) pies

AIRY COCONUT CREAM WHIPPED TOPPING

In a high-speed blender, blend together the coconut meat, coconut cream, agar paste, powdered xylitol, sunflower lecithin, vanilla and salt until smooth. Add the melted coconut oil and blend again until well combined. Transfer the mixture to a shallow container and chill in the fridge overnight or for a minimum of 12 hours. Meanwhile, start making the tart crusts, as they also need time to set. This whipped topping will last in the fridge for 3 days or up to 1 month in the freezer and is a wonderful pie topper.

(continued)

Airy Coconut Cream Whipped Topping

1 cup (160 g) chopped young coconut meat

½ cup (120 ml) Coconut Cream (page 27)

¼ cup (60 ml) Agar Paste (page 31)

¼ cup (49 g) powdered xylitol (see Prep Notes on page 18)

1 tsp sunflower lecithin powder

6 drops vanilla extract, Medicine Flower brand preferred

⅛ tsp Himalayan salt

½ cup (120 ml) melted virgin coconut oil

BANANA CREAM PIE WITH GINGERBREAD CRUST
(continued)

GINGERBREAD TART CRUSTS

In a food processor, process the almonds, activated oat flour, mesquite powder (if using), coconut sugar, cinnamon, cloves, allspice and salt together until the mixture resembles coarse flour. Add the melted coconut oil, coconut nectar and ginger, and process the mixture again until the batter starts sticking together.

The tart pans do not need to be lined since we do not use sticky ingredients, such as dried fruit. Once the crust is set, it will pop right out of the mold. Using your fingers, divide the crust mixture equally between two 4-inch (10-cm) round tart pans with a removable bottom and use a small spoon to even out the bottom of the crust. Set them aside at room temperature while you make the filling.

BANANA CREAM FILLING

In a high-speed blender, blend together the banana, coconut meat, coconut cream, agave, sunflower lecithin and salt until smooth. Add the melted coconut oil and blend again until combined. Pour the filling into each tart crust, leaving room at the top for a layer of bananas, and gently pat the pies on the counter to remove any air bubbles. Slice the banana into coins and create a layer of bananas on top of the filling. Chill the pies in the fridge or freezer for a few hours to set.

ASSEMBLY

Remove the pies from the fridge or freezer and the airy coconut whipped cream topping from the fridge. If the whipped topping is quite firm, allow it to sit at room temperature until it's soft enough for piping. If it is too soft, chill it in the freezer for 10 to 20 minutes to firm up. Once the coconut whip is at the right consistency for piping, whip it with a fork. Remove the pies from the tart tins before garnishing.

Fit a Wilton 1M piping tip to a piping bag and fill the piping bag with the airy coconut cream whipped topping. Hold the piping bag vertically above the pie and pipe dollops of airy coconut whipped cream on top of the pie until the entire pie is covered. Serve immediately. The pies will keep in the fridge for up to 3 days or in the freezer for 1 month.

Gingerbread Tart Crusts

¾ cup (97.5 g) soaked and dehydrated almonds (see Prep Notes on page 20)

½ cup (65 g) Activated Oat Flour (page 28)

1 tbsp (8 g) mesquite powder (optional)

1 tbsp (10 g) coconut sugar

½ tsp ground cinnamon

⅛ tsp ground cloves

⅛ tsp ground allspice

⅛ tsp Himalayan salt

3 tbsp (45 ml) melted virgin coconut oil

1 tbsp (15 ml) coconut nectar

1 tsp grated fresh ginger

Banana Cream Filling

⅔ cup (100 g) chopped fresh, ripe banana (1 small banana)

½ cup (80 g) chopped young coconut meat

¼ cup + 2 tbsp (90 ml) Coconut Cream (page 27)

3 tbsp (64 g) light-amber agave

1 tsp sunflower lecithin powder

Pinch of Himalayan salt

¼ cup + 2 tbsp (90 ml) melted virgin coconut oil

1 ripe banana, to top

CREAMY ICE CREAM WITHOUT THE DAIRY

It is possible to make creamy and delicious ice cream without dairy! Instead, we use a base of cashews and/ or coconut meat along with other ingredients. This chapter includes three different flavors of ice cream plus an ice-cream cake and ice-cream cookie sandwiches. These recipes are popular with the kiddos and a wonderful summer treat.

As a child, I celebrated my birthday every year with a Dairy Queen™ ice-cream cake, but since adopting a vegan diet, I can no longer enjoy them. So, I took on the challenge of creating a raw vegan version; the Berries and Cream Coconut Ice-Cream Cake (page 127) is made with berry ice cream on a mulberry lime crust with berry jam and frosted with a coconut frosting. You'll have a lot of fun decorating this one.

Countertop ice-cream makers have become very popular in recent years; I highly recommend using one—it will save you a lot of time when making ice cream. If you do not have an ice-cream maker, I have provided instructions on how to make ice cream without one.

VANILLA BEAN ICE CREAM

Yield: About 3 cups (710 ml)

This recipe is simple and delicious, wonderful on its own or as an addition to other desserts. We use Vanilla Bean Ice Cream on a few recipes in this book, including the Pecan Pie with Rosemary and Orange (page 107) and the Chocolate Chip Ice-Cream Cookie Sandwiches (page 130). If serving alone, top with the Ginger Caramel Sauce (page 159) or Chocolate Sauce (page 154), or both! If unavailable locally, vanilla beans are easily sourced on Amazon. You will want to use them if you can; they produce a wonderful flavor and add some texture to enhance the aesthetic.

In a high-speed blender, blend together the cashews, Brazil nut milk, agave, sunflower lecithin, vanilla (if using extract instead of the bean) and salt until smooth. Add the melted coconut oil and blend again until combined. If using the vanilla bean, slice it down the middle and remove the seeds with the tip of your knife by scraping the bean. Add them to the blender and blend again on low speed for a few seconds to incorporate the vanilla bean seeds.

If using an ice-cream maker, prepare the device per the manufacturer's instructions. Pour the mixture into the ice-cream maker and follow the manufacturer's instructions. Once it's processed, the ice cream is ready to serve, but if you would like it firmer, transfer the mixture to a container and chill in the freezer for a few hours.

If you do not have an ice-cream maker, pour the mixture into a large, flat container or pan and chill it in the freezer for 45 minutes. Remove the pan from the freezer and stir with a fork, moving the frozen mixture away from the edges. Repeat the process of stirring the mixture with a fork, moving the frozen mixture away from the edges, every 20 to 30 minutes for an additional 3 to 4 hours, until it is almost completely frozen. This process will aerate the ice cream.

Store the ice cream in the freezer. It will last for months.

1½ cups (210 g) raw cashews, soaked for 2 hours and rinsed

1 cup (240 ml) Brazil Nut Milk (page 25)

⅓ cup (107 ml) light-amber agave

1½ tsp (scant 4 g) sunflower lecithin powder

1 vanilla bean, or 8 drops vanilla extract, Medicine Flower brand preferred

⅛ tsp Himalayan salt

¼ cup (60 ml) melted virgin coconut oil

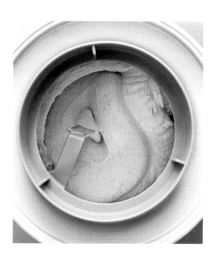

MINT CHOCOLATE CHIP ICE CREAM

Yield: 3 cups (720 ml)
Nut-free

Mint and chocolate are some of my favorite flavor combinations. Food-grade peppermint essential oil is used to add a strong minty flavor to the ice cream, making it super fresh, and the Candied Cacao Nibs (page 152) add a nice crunch and texture. This recipe is 100% nut-free, made with a base of coconut as a nut-free cream alternative. The texture is unreal! This recipe uses young coconut meat, but refer to the Substitution List (page 160) for other non-dairy alternatives. You can serve this ice cream with Chocolate Sauce (page 154).

In a high-speed blender, blend together the coconut cream, coconut meat, coconut nectar, sunflower lecithin, spirulina, vanilla, peppermint essential oil and salt until smooth. Add the softened coconut butter and blend again until smooth.

If using an ice-cream maker, prepare the device per the manufacturer's instructions. Pour the mixture into the ice-cream maker and follow the manufacturer's instructions. At the end of processing, slowly add the candied cacao nibs. Once it's processed, the ice cream is ready to serve, but if you would like it firmer, transfer the mixture to a container and chill it in the freezer for a few hours.

If you do not have an ice-cream maker, pour the mixture into a large, flat container or pan and chill it in the freezer for 45 minutes. Remove the pan from the freezer and stir with a fork, moving the frozen mixture away from the edges. Repeat the process of stirring the mixture with a fork, moving the frozen mixture away from the edges, every 20 to 30 minutes for 5 to 6 hours, until it resembles ice cream. This process will aerate the ice cream. Stir in the candied cacao nibs at the end, while the mixture is still soft enough to mix but almost frozen. For a firmer texture, chill in the freezer for 8 hours.

Store the ice cream in the freezer. It will last for months.

1½ cups (360 ml) Coconut Cream (page 27)

1 cup (160 g) chopped young coconut meat

½ cup (120 ml) coconut nectar

1½ tsp (scant 4 g) sunflower lecithin powder

1–2 tsp (2–4 g) spirulina, moringa or matcha powder, for color

6 drops vanilla extract, Medicine Flower brand preferred

4 drops food-grade peppermint essential oil

¼ tsp Himalayan salt

¼ cup (60 ml) softened Coconut Butter (page 31)

½ cup (62.5 g) Candied Cacao Nibs (page 152)

PRO TIP: This ice cream takes a little longer to freeze in the ice-cream maker, or if processing it manually, than the other ice cream recipes in this chapter. The patience is worth it; the result is an ultra creamy, dairy-free, nut-free coconut-based ice cream.

DECADENT CHOCOLATE ICE CREAM

This is the ultimate chocolate ice cream recipe! Espresso powder is added to boost the chocolate flavor, but is optional. Sunflower lecithin powder makes a big difference in this recipe, as it emulsifies the fats and the liquids, resulting in an extra-creamy base. Make sure to have made some Hazelnut Praline (page 105) before starting this recipe.

Yield: About 3 cups (710 ml)

In a high-speed blender, blend together the cashews, almond milk, coconut nectar, cacao powder, sunflower lecithin, espresso powder (if using), salt and vanilla until smooth. Add the melted cacao paste and blend for a few seconds until combined.

If using an ice-cream maker, prepare the device per the manufacturer's instructions. Pour the mixture into the ice-cream maker and follow the manufacturer's instructions. At the end of processing, slowly add the hazelnut praline. If the hazelnut praline is chunky, chop or blitz it first in a food processor to prevent it getting stuck in the ice-cream maker. Once it's processed, this ice cream is nice and thick and ready to serve immediately. To serve, top with more chopped hazelnut praline and dried rose petals (if using). If you would like a firmer ice cream, transfer the mixture to a container and chill it in the freezer for a few hours.

If you do not have an ice-cream maker, pour the mixture into a large, flat container or pan and chill it in the freezer for 45 minutes. Remove the pan from the freezer, manually fold in the hazelnut praline and then stir with a fork and move the frozen mixture away from the edges. Repeat the process of stirring the mixture with a fork, moving the frozen mixture away from the edges, every 20 to 30 minutes for an additional 3 to 4 hours, until it is almost completely frozen. This process will aerate the ice cream. To serve, top with more chopped hazelnut praline and dried rose petals (if using).

Store the ice cream in the freezer. It will last for months. Once stored in the freezer, this ice cream is much firmer because of the added cacao paste; it will require thawing before serving.

1 cup (140 g) raw cashews, soaked for 2 hours and rinsed

2 cups (480 ml) Almond Milk (page 24)

½ cup (120 ml) coconut nectar

⅓ cup (32 g) cacao powder

1½ tsp (scant 4 g) sunflower lecithin powder

¼ tsp espresso powder (optional)

⅛ tsp Himalayan salt

12 drops vanilla extract, Medicine Flower brand preferred

75 g chopped cacao paste, melted

⅔ cup (85 g) chopped Hazelnut Praline (page 105), plus more for garnish

Garnishes

Dried food-grade rose petals (optional)

BERRIES AND CREAM COCONUT ICE-CREAM CAKE

Yield: One 6-inch (15-cm) cake

Ice-cream cakes are a fun way to celebrate any occasion. This is not your traditional ice-cream cake; it's a healthier version made with a dehydrated jam and berry coconut ice cream filling on top of a mulberry lime crust, finished with Coconut Frosting (page 148). It's light and refreshing, perfect for the warmer weather. For frosting the cake, you will require cake decorating tools, such as piping bags, an offset spatula, a pastry scraper (optional), a cake board and a cake turntable (optional). Check out the Substitutions List (page 160) for options on swapping out the dried white mulberries.

MIXED BERRY JAM

In a food processor, combine the thawed mixed berries, coconut nectar, lime zest and salt and pulse until a chunky texture is achieved. Transfer the mixture to a stainless-steel or glass bowl, place in the bottom of your dehydrator or on a lower tray and dehydrate at 115°F (46°C) for 18 to 24 hours, or until reduced and thick. Transfer the jam to a sealed container and place in the fridge for a few hours to thicken up further. Once cooled, it will resemble a thick, chunky jam.

MULBERRY LIME CRUST

In a food processor, process the almonds, coconut, activated oat flour, lucuma powder, coconut sugar and salt together until a fine crumble is created. Add the mulberries, melted coconut oil and lime zest, and process until the batter starts sticking together.

Line the inside of one 6-inch (15-cm) cake ring with a cake collar or acetate sheet and place the cake ring on a lined cutting board or tray. Press the crust mixture into the bottom of the cake ring firmly, using your fingers, until an even layer is achieved. Set the crust aside while you make the filling.

(continued)

Mixed Berry Jam

2 cups (290 g) frozen mixed berries, thawed (measured before thawing)

⅓ cup (80 ml) coconut nectar

1 tsp lime zest

⅛ tsp Himalayan salt

Mulberry Lime Crust

½ cup (65 g) soaked and dehydrated almonds (see Prep Notes on page 20)

¼ cup (20 g) medium-shred unsweetened dried coconut

¼ cup (33 g) Activated Oat Flour (page 28)

1 tbsp (7.5 g) lucuma powder

2 tbsp (20 g) coconut sugar

⅛ tsp Himalayan salt

¼ cup (28 g) dried white mulberries, soaked for 20 minutes and strained

2 tbsp (30 ml) melted virgin coconut oil

1 tsp lime zest

BERRIES AND CREAM COCONUT
ICE-CREAM CAKE (continued)

MIXED BERRY ICE CREAM

Before starting the berry ice cream, make sure to have a batch of the mixed berry jam ready. In a high-speed blender, blend together the coconut milk, cashews, freeze-dried berries, young coconut meat, coconut nectar, sunflower lecithin, lime juice and salt until smooth. Add the melted coconut oil and blend again until combined.

Place the mixed berry jam in the center of the crust, leaving a scant ¼ inch (0.5 cm) of space around the outside edge to ensure the jam does not leak from the cake. Pour the berry ice cream mixture into the cake ring on top of the berry jam. Pat the cake ring on the counter to remove any air bubbles from the filling and even out the mixture. Chill the cake in the freezer for a minimum of 12 hours or overnight. The cake should be completely frozen before frosting.

ASSEMBLY

Remove the frosting from the fridge and check to see if it is firm to the touch; if it is soft, chill it in the freezer for 10 to 20 minutes, remove it from the freezer and stir it around, whipping it up. If it is too firm, allow it to sit at room temperature to soften.

Prepare your area for cake decorating by gathering the following equipment and tools: a cake turntable (optional), a 6-inch (15-cm) cake board, masking tape (optional), two piping bags, an Ateco 1M piping tip, a small offset spatula and a pastry scraper.

Secure the cake board to the cake turntable (if using) with a piece of masking tape underneath the cake board. Fill a piping bag with the coconut frosting and cut off the tip to create a ⅜-inch (1-cm)-diameter hole. Place a dollop of frosting in the center of the board and the ice-cream cake on top, securing it to the cake board.

Mixed Berry Ice Cream

1¼ cups (295 ml) Coconut Milk (page 27)

1 cup (140 g) raw cashews, soaked for 2 hours and rinsed

1 cup (40 g) mixed freeze-dried berries (I used blueberries and strawberries; measured before thawing)

½ cup (80 g) young coconut meat

½ cup (120 ml) coconut nectar

1½ tsp (scant 4 g) sunflower lecithin powder

1 tbsp (15 ml) fresh lime juice

¼ tsp Himalayan salt

¼ cup (60 ml) melted virgin coconut oil

Assembly

1 batch Coconut Frosting (page 148)

Fresh blackberries and blueberries

Fresh mint leaves

Using the piping bag filled with coconut frosting, create a layer of frosting on the outside of the ice-cream cake, starting from the bottom in a circular motion, until the entire exterior of the cake is covered. Create a layer of frosting on top as well. Using a small offset spatula, smooth the frosting vertically from bottom to top.

Using your pastry scraper at a vertical angle, gently scrape the sides of the cake while moving your cake turntable (if using) to even out the layer. If you don't have a pastry scraper, feel free to use an offset spatula to smooth the frosting. Be careful not to remove too much frosting. Smooth the top with a small offset spatula and remove excess frosting from the edges.

Garnish the cake with fresh blackberries, blueberries and fresh mint leaves.

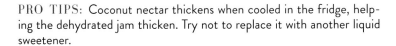

PRO TIPS: Coconut nectar thickens when cooled in the fridge, helping the dehydrated jam thicken. Try not to replace it with another liquid sweetener.

Sunflower lecithin powder is critical in reducing the ice crystals in the berry ice cream filling; try not to omit this, either.

CHOCOLATE CHIP ICE-CREAM COOKIE SANDWICHES

These chocolate chip cookies will surprise you and anyone you serve them to because of their "baked" texture from the dehydrator. It's hard not to eat the entire batter before it makes it to the dehydrator. Make sure to have fresh almond pulp and Candied Cacao Nibs (page 152) prepared for this recipe.

Yield: 6 ice-cream cookie sandwiches

CHOCOLATE CHIP COOKIES

In a food processor, process the coconut, activated oat flour, coconut sugar, ground flax and salt together until the mixture forms a fine crumble. Add the almond pulp, apricots, almond butter, coconut nectar and vanilla, and process again until the cookie dough starts sticking together. Last, add the candied cacao nibs and pulse until they are incorporated into the batter.

Secure a piece of parchment paper or a reusable dehydrator sheet to the countertop, using masking tape. Place the cookie dough on top of the parchment and place another piece of parchment paper or reusable dehydrator sheet on top. Press the dough ball down firmly before using a rolling pin to smooth it out. Roll out the dough to about ½ inch (1.3 cm) thick.

Form the cookies with a small round cookie cutter and transfer each cookie to a mesh-lined dehydrator tray by using an offset spatula and scooping them from underneath. Repeat this process until 12 cookies are formed.

Dehydrate at 115°F (46°C) for 12 hours, or until crispy on the outside but still soft on the inside. Allow the cookies to cool before assembling with ice cream.

ASSEMBLY

Using a small ice-cream scoop, place a scoop of ice cream in the middle of one cookie and place another cookie on top. Only assemble this recipe right before serving or store the components separately. The cookies will keep in the fridge for up to 1 week and the ice cream will keep in the freezer for months.

Chocolate Chip Cookies

1 cup (80 g) medium-shred unsweetened dried coconut

¼ cup (33 g) Activated Oat Flour (page 28)

¼ cup (40 g) coconut sugar

2 tbsp (14 g) ground golden flax (see Prep Notes on page 18)

Pinch of Himalayan salt

¾ cup (149 g) packed almond pulp (left over from making Almond Milk; see page 24)

½ cup (64 g) dried apricots, soaked for 20 minutes, drained and chopped

2 tbsp (32 g) almond butter

2 tbsp (30 ml) coconut nectar

8 drops vanilla extract, Medicine Flower brand preferred

⅓ cup (41 g) Candied Cacao Nibs (page 152)

Assembly

1 batch Vanilla Bean Ice Cream (page 120)

PRO TIP: The cookies will decrease in size as they dehydrate, so do not roll out the dough too thinly.

DELIGHTFUL SLICES AND BARS

These slices and bars recipes make wonderful snacks; they freeze well, so make big batches and you'll always have some on hand.

The Double Chocolate Red Velvet Brownies (page 137) are my favorite recipe in this chapter. I wanted to create a gooey raw brownie, so I used real red beets to provide a moist base; no dehydrator is required as these are set in the freezer. Everyone who tried these could not believe they were made with beets; I hope you love them as much as I do!

If you want to be transported to a tropical island, the Hawaiian Sunshine Crumble Squares (page 143) will do just that with tropical flavors including macadamia nuts, mango, pineapple and coconut. These have become my husband's all-time favorite.

TIGER NUT TAHINI SLICE

Yield: 30 to 33 slices
Nut-free

Tiger nuts are not a nut at all; they are a tuber that grows on the end of the yellow nutsedge plant. Tubers are storage systems for plants that hold nutrients and water. The most commonly known tubers are potatoes. Whole tiger nuts are challenging to work with, so in this recipe, we use tiger nut flour and skinned tiger nuts, as they blend and process much more manageably. Tiger nuts are easily sourced online on Amazon or at Nuts.com® or in the baking aisle of your local organic grocery or health food store. You will require a good blender for this recipe to blend the tiger nuts smooth. If you do not have a high-speed blender, soak the tiger nuts for 8 hours. If you are unable to source them, check out the Substitutions List (page 160) for other alternatives.

TIGER NUT OAT CRUST

In a food processor, process the tiger nut flour, rolled oats, mesquite powder and salt together until the mixture resembles coarse flour. Add the coconut nectar, melted coconut oil and vanilla, and process until combined and the batter starts sticking together.

Line an 8-inch (20-cm) square baking pan with parchment paper and, using your hands, press the crust batter into the bottom of the pan to create an even, thick layer. Using the back of a spoon, firmly smooth out the layer. Set the crust aside at room temperature while you make the tiger nut tahini cream.

TIGER NUT TAHINI CREAM

In a high-speed blender, blend together the skinned tiger nuts, water, tahini, coconut nectar and vanilla until smooth. Add the melted coconut oil and blend again until combined. Pour the tiger nut tahini cream onto the crust and pat the pan on the counter to even out the layer and remove any air bubbles. Transfer the pan to the freezer to set for a minimum of 4 hours before adding the dark chocolate ganache.

(continued)

Tiger Nut Oat Crust

1 cup (120 g) tiger nut flour

1 cup (80 g) gluten-free rolled oats

¼ cup (32 g) mesquite powder or
¼ cup (30 g) lucuma powder

⅛ tsp Himalayan salt

¼ cup (60 ml) coconut nectar

3 tbsp (45 ml) melted virgin coconut oil

10 drops vanilla extract, Medicine Flower brand preferred (optional)

Tiger Nut Tahini Cream

1 cup (160 g) skinned tiger nuts

¾ cup (180 ml) water

¼ cup (60 g) tahini

¼ cup (60 ml) coconut nectar

6 drops vanilla extract, Medicine Flower brand preferred (optional)

¼ cup + 2 tbsp (90 ml) melted virgin coconut oil

TIGER NUT TAHINI SLICE
(continued)

ASSEMBLY

Make the dark chocolate ganache and pour it into the pan. Tap the pan on the counter to even out the layer. The ganache will start setting quickly on the frozen filling, so work fast. Use an offset spatula to even out the layer, if required. Chill in the freezer for a minimum of 8 hours or overnight, until firm.

Remove from the freezer and trim the edges with a knife to create a clean line on all four sides. Slice into 2 x 1–inch (5 x 2.5–cm) bars (you can use a ruler to mark each cut with a knife). Make sure to clean your knife in between each slice.

Line a cutting board or tray with parchment paper and transfer the bars to the prepared surface. Place the bars back in the freezer to firm up for 30 minutes before decorating (if they are getting soft). Make or melt the enrobing dark chocolate and transfer the melted chocolate to a piping bag or squeeze bottle for decoration. If using a piping bag, cut off the end to create a small hole.

Drizzle the bars with the chocolate and sprinkle the tops with a little fleur de sel (if using). Serve immediately or store in the fridge for up to 5 days or in the freezer for up to 1 month.

PRO TIPS: If the slices are difficult to cut straight out of the freezer, you may need to thaw the pan for 15 to 20 minutes before slicing. Warm your knife and clean the knife in between each slice for a sharp, even slice.

Fleur de sel is a finishing salt and optional, but looks really pretty on these slices and balances the sweetness.

Assembly

1 batch Dark Chocolate Ganache (page 153)

½ batch Enrobing Dark Chocolate (page 156)

Fleur de sel (optional)

DOUBLE CHOCOLATE RED VELVET BROWNIES

We use fresh beets in this recipe to create a red velvet appeal, moisten the brownies and provide an extra boost of nutrition. This recipe is in my top five all-time favorites; the result is a tender, delicious brownie. The candied nibbed walnuts are added for crunch and flavor, but they are a great recipe on their own as well, for a snack or ice cream topper!

Yield: 16 brownies

CANDIED NIBBED WALNUTS

In a bowl, combine the walnuts, cacao nibs, coconut sugar, coconut nectar, vanilla and salt. Spread the mixture on a lined dehydrator tray and dehydrate at 115°F (46°C) for 24 hours. The mixture will be sticky but will have a crunchy texture once cooled. Place the candied walnuts in the freezer to crisp up before use.

RED VELVET BROWNIES

In a high-speed blender, blend together the beets and dates to form a puree. In a food processor, process the cacao powder, coconut, almonds, walnuts, coconut sugar and salt together until a coarse flour forms. Be careful not to overprocess the mixture into a fine flour; some texture should remain.

Add the beet mixture, melted coconut oil and vanilla to the food processor, and process until the mixture is combined and starts sticking together. Add the chopped candied nibbed walnuts and pulse until they are incorporated. The batter will be very sticky and you may have to stir in the candied walnuts by hand using a spatula.

Line an 8-inch (20-cm) square baking pan with parchment paper and, using your hands, press the brownie batter into the bottom of the pan to create an even, thick layer. Using the back of a spoon, firmly smooth out the layer.

(continued)

Candied Nibbed Walnuts

2 cups (200 g) raw walnuts, soaked for 4 hours and rinsed

¼ cup (30 g) cacao nibs

¼ cup (40 g) coconut sugar

2 tbsp (30 ml) coconut nectar

6 drops vanilla extract, Medicine Flower brand preferred

Pinch of Himalayan salt

Red Velvet Brownies

1 cup (165 g) peeled and chopped red beets

11 large Medjool dates, soaked to soften and pitted

¾ cup (72 g) cacao powder

1 cup (80 g) medium-shred unsweetened dried coconut

1 cup (130 g) soaked and dehydrated almonds (see Prep Notes on page 20)

¾ cup (75 g) soaked and dehydrated walnuts (see Prep Notes on page 20)

¼ cup (40 g) coconut sugar

¼ tsp Himalayan salt

2 tbsp (30 ml) melted virgin coconut oil

10 drops vanilla extract, Medicine Flower brand preferred

¾ cup (111 g) chopped Candied Nibbed Walnuts

DOUBLE CHOCOLATE RED VELVET BROWNIES (continued)

ASSEMBLY

Before adding the dark chocolate ganache, have the white chocolate sauce made and ready to use as we are using this as a marble decoration on top. Pour the dark chocolate ganache on top of the brownie mixture and pat the pan on the counter to release any air bubbles and even out the mixture.

Transfer the white chocolate sauce to a squeeze bottle or piping bag and create horizontal lines approximately ⅜ inch (1 cm) apart, starting from one side of the pan to the other, until there are even lines across the entire ganache layer. Using a toothpick or wooden skewer, graze only the top of the lines from one end to another in the opposite direction, alternating from top to bottom, creating a beautiful design on top.

Chill the brownies in the freezer overnight or for a minimum of 8 hours, until firm. Remove the pan from the freezer and slice into 2-inch (5-cm) squares (you can use a ruler to mark each cut with a knife). Allow to thaw and serve immediately or store in the freezer for up to 1 month or the fridge for up to 3 days. They won't last long in the fridge because of the fresh beets, but they store well in the freezer.

PRO TIP: When choosing beets for this recipe, choose the ones smaller in size. The larger the beet, the woodier it tastes. Smaller beets are sweeter.

Assembly

1 batch Dark Chocolate Ganache (page 153)

1 batch White Chocolate Sauce (page 158)

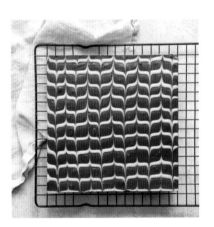

STRAWBERRY ROSE PISTACHIO CREAM SLICE

The pistachio, rose and cardamom flavors in this recipe are inspired by a popular dessert called Persian Love Cake. These are pretty and fun to decorate. Almond brings out pistachio's flavor beautifully. Rose is optional but provides a nice punch. Make sure to have some Rich Vanilla Cream Frosting (page 149) prepared to create an elegant garnish on these slices.

Yield: 30 to 33 bars

ALMOND STRAWBERRY CRUST

In a food processor, process the almonds, activated oat flour, freeze-dried strawberries, coconut sugar, lucuma powder, cardamom and salt together until the almonds are broken down into a small crumble. Do not overprocess the crust, as there should be some texture present. Add the melted coconut oil, almond butter and vanilla, and process until combined and the batter starts sticking together.

Line an 8-inch (20-cm) square baking pan with parchment paper and, using your hands, press the crust batter into the bottom of the pan to create an even, thick layer. Using the back of a spoon, firmly smooth out the layer. Set the crust aside at room temperature while you make the strawberry rose cream.

(continued)

Almond Strawberry Crust

1½ cups (195 g) soaked and dehydrated almonds (see Prep Notes on page 20)

¾ cup (98 g) Activated Oat Flour (page 28)

½ cup (18 g) sliced freeze-dried strawberries

¼ cup (40 g) coconut sugar

3 tbsp (22.5 g) lucuma powder

¼ tsp ground cardamom

⅛ tsp Himalayan salt

2 tbsp (30 ml) melted virgin coconut oil

2 tbsp (32 g) almond butter

6 drops vanilla extract, Medicine Flower brand preferred

STRAWBERRY ROSE CREAM

In a high-speed blender, blend together the cashews, almond milk, freeze-dried strawberries, agave, lemon juice, sunflower lecithin, beet powder, salt and rose extract until smooth. Add the melted coconut oil and blend again until combined.

Pour the strawberry cream layer onto the crust and pat the pan on the counter to even out the layer and remove any air bubbles. Transfer the pan to the freezer to set for a minimum of 4 hours before adding the pistachio cream.

PISTACHIO CREAM

In a high-speed blender, blend together the cashews, pistachio milk, agave, sunflower lecithin, salt, vanilla and almond extract (if using) until smooth. Add the melted coconut oil and blend again until combined. Remove the pan from the freezer, pour the pistachio cream on top of the strawberry rose cream and pat the pan on the counter to even out the layer and remove any air bubbles. Chill in the freezer for 8 hours or overnight, until firm.

ASSEMBLY

Remove from the freezer and trim the edges with a knife to create a clean line on all four sides. Slice into 2 x 1–inch (5 x 2.5–cm) bars (you can use a ruler to mark each cut with a knife). Make sure to clean your knife in between each slice.

Line a cutting board or tray with parchment paper and transfer the bars to the prepared surface. Place them back in the freezer to firm up for 30 minutes before decorating (if they are getting soft). During this time, remove the vanilla frosting from the fridge to check the consistency for piping. If the frosting is too soft, chill in the freezer for 10 to 20 minutes to firm up, then whip with a spoon.

Fit an Ateco 125 piping tip to a piping bag and fill the piping bag with the vanilla frosting. Above each slice, hold the piping bag horizontally, so the piping tip is in a vertical position with the wide angle of the tip at the bottom. Squeeze the piping bag slowly and, using even pressure, create a ribbon effect on top of each slice. Garnish with dried rose petals and crushed pistachios. Serve immediately or store in the fridge for up to 5 days or in the freezer for up to 1 month.

PRO TIP: If the slices are difficult to cut out of the freezer, you may need to thaw the bars for 15 to 20 minutes before slicing. Warm your knife and clean it in between each slice.

Strawberry Rose Cream

1 cup (140 g) raw cashews, soaked for 2 hours and rinsed

½ cup (120 ml) Almond Milk (page 24)

¼ cup + 2 tbsp (13.5 g) freeze-dried sliced strawberries

¼ cup (85 g) light-amber agave

1½ tsp (8 ml) fresh lemon juice

1½ tsp (scant 4 g) sunflower lecithin powder

¼ tsp beet powder

⅛ tsp Himalayan salt

6 drops rose extract, Medicine Flower brand preferred, or any rose flavor extract

¼ cup (60 ml) melted virgin coconut oil

Pistachio Cream

1 cup (140 g) raw cashews, soaked for 2 hours and rinsed

½ cup (120 ml) Pistachio Milk (page 26)

¼ cup (85 g) light-amber agave

1½ tsp (scant 4 g) sunflower lecithin powder

⅛ tsp Himalayan salt

6 drops vanilla extract, Medicine Flower brand preferred

2 drops almond extract, Medicine Flower brand preferred (optional)

¼ cup (60 ml) melted virgin coconut oil

Assembly

1 batch Rich Vanilla Cream Frosting (page 149)

Dried food-grade rose petals

Crushed pistachios

HAWAIIAN SUNSHINE CRUMBLE SQUARES

The flavors of this recipe will make you feel like you're in a tropical paradise on a beach. This is a fun recipe to enjoy for breakfast or a snack. Don't omit the sunflower lecithin powder in this recipe; it's key to the tropical cream's creamy consistency. This recipe uses young coconut meat, but check out the Substitutions List (page 160) for other options.

Yield: 17 bars

MACADAMIA TAHINI OAT CRUMBLE

In a food processor, process the macadamia nuts, rolled oats, shredded coconut and salt together until the mixture resembles a crumble. Add the agave, tahini, lime zest and vanilla, and process again until combined. Do not overprocess the mixture; it should retain a crumble consistency.

Spread the crumble on a lined dehydrator tray and dehydrate at 115°F (46°C) for 16 to 18 hours, or until fully dry. Transfer the crumble to the freezer to crisp up until ready to use.

MACADAMIA OAT CRUST

In a food processor, process the macadamia nuts, rolled oats, shredded coconut and salt together until the mixture resembles coarse flour. Add the agave, tahini, melted coconut oil, lime zest and vanilla, and process again until the batter sticks together. Do not overprocess, since the macadamia nuts will release oil very quickly.

Line an 8-inch (20-cm) square baking pan with parchment paper and, using your hands, press the crust batter into the bottom of the pan to create an even, thick layer. Using the back of a spoon, firmly smooth out the layer. Set the crust aside at room temperature while you make the tropical cream.

(continued)

Macadamia Tahini Oat Crumble

1 cup (135 g) raw macadamia nuts, soaked for 2 hours and rinsed

1 cup (80 g) gluten-free rolled oats

⅔ cup (50 g) medium-shred unsweetened dried coconut

⅛ tsp Himalayan salt

¼ cup (85 g) light-amber agave

2 tbsp (30 g) tahini

1 tbsp (6 g) lime zest

6 drops vanilla extract, Medicine Flower brand preferred

Macadamia Oat Crust

1 cup (125 g) raw macadamia nuts

1 cup (80 g) gluten-free rolled oats

⅓ cup (25 g) medium-shred unsweetened dried coconut

⅛ tsp Himalayan salt

2 tbsp (43 ml) light-amber agave

2 tbsp (30 g) tahini

2 tbsp (30 ml) melted virgin coconut oil

1 tsp lime zest

3 drops vanilla extract, Medicine Flower brand preferred

TROPICAL CREAM

In a high-speed blender, blend together the mango, pineapple, coconut meat, coconut butter, agave, lemon juice, sunflower lecithin and salt until smooth. Add the melted coconut oil and blend again until combined. Pour the tropical cream filling on top of the crust and pat the pan on the counter to even out the layer and remove any air bubbles.

ASSEMBLY

Remove the crumble from the freezer; if the pieces are large, blitz the crumble in a food processor until broken down. Add the crumble evenly as a layer on top of the tropical cream filling, pressing the crumble into the cream so the crumble sets in the filling.

Chill the pan in the freezer for a minimum of 6 hours to set. Remove from the freezer and slice into 2-inch (5-cm) squares. Serve immediately or store in the freezer for up to 1 month or the fridge for up to 3 days.

Tropical Cream

1½ cups (225 g) frozen mango, thawed (measured before thawing)

1 cup (135 g) frozen pineapple, thawed (measured before thawing)

¾ cup (120 g) chopped young coconut meat

¼ cup (60 g) softened Coconut Butter (page 31)

¼ cup (85 g) light-amber agave

2 tbsp (30 ml) fresh lemon juice

1½ tsp (scant 4 g) sunflower lecithin powder

⅛ tsp Himalayan salt

2 tbsp (30 ml) melted virgin coconut oil

RAW FROSTINGS, GARNISHES AND FINISHING TOUCHES

No raw dessert cookbook would be complete without a section for raw frostings and garnishes. This chapter is full of my go-to, tried-and-true raw recipes. There are a variety of frostings, including a nut-free version with a coconut base (page 148), a vanilla frosting (page 149), a chocolate frosting (page 150) and a probiotic-rich cultured frosting (page 151). We use these in various recipes throughout the book, but feel free to switch those up in the recipes with other frostings in this chapter.

Finishing touches and garnishes are the perfect recipes to elevate your desserts. We also add these components, such as the Candied Cacao Nibs (page 152), which is my raw version of chocolate chips, to lots of recipes in this book.

There is a recipe for raw Chocolate Sauce (page 154) that we add to crêpes, ice cream and cakes; it pairs well with many desserts in this book. Have you ever wondered how pastry chefs achieve a perfect chocolate drip on a cake? I include my Dark Chocolate Ganache recipe (page 153) to help you mimic those results!

COCONUT FROSTING

Yield: About 4 cups (960 ml)
Nut-free

This recipe is totally nut-free and one of my favorite low-sugar frostings. Use this to frost cakes and cupcakes, or as a garnish. Add vibrant-colored superfood powders (such as spirulina or matcha powder for green, beet powder for pink or even ground turmeric for yellow) to color the frosting naturally and modify it to suit your favorite flavors. This recipe is sweetened with low-glycemic xylitol, but check out the Substitutions List (page 160) for other alternatives. We use this frosting to frost the Berries and Cream Coconut Ice-Cream Cake (page 127), on top of the Avocado Key Lime Pies with Coconut Cream (page 112), on top of the Blackberry Ginger Lime Zebra Cheesecake (page 61) and as a garnish on top of the carrot cake on page 76.

In a high-speed blender, blend together the coconut meat, coconut milk, xylitol, sunflower lecithin (if using), lemon juice, vanilla and salt until smooth. Add the melted coconut oil and blend again until combined.

Transfer the frosting to a shallow container and chill in the fridge for 8 to 12 hours. Depending on your environment and fridge temperature, the setting time will vary. When the frosting is set, it should be firm to the touch. This frosting usually sets really fast. This frosting freezes well in a sealed container for a couple of months. Thaw it in the fridge for 2 days before use.

PRO TIP: Working with raw frostings and getting it to the perfect consistency for piping and frosting a cake takes practice. If the coconut frosting is too firm, let it sit at room temperature for 2 hours before use. This batch will frost an entire 4-inch (10-cm) three-layer cake, as well as the 6-inch (15-cm) Berries and Cream Coconut Ice-Cream Cake (page 127).

2 cups (333 g) packed chopped young coconut meat

1 cup (240 ml) Coconut Milk (page 27)

¼ cup + 2 tbsp (73 g) powdered xylitol (see Prep Notes on page 18)

1 tbsp (7.5 g) sunflower lecithin powder (optional)

2 tbsp (30 ml) fresh lemon juice

16 drops vanilla extract, Medicine Flower brand preferred

⅛ tsp Himalayan salt

½ cup (120 ml) melted virgin coconut oil

RICH VANILLA CREAM FROSTING

Yield: About 2 cups (475 ml)

This is a wonderful cream-colored vanilla frosting to use as a garnish. It is very smooth and rich and produces a professional-looking result. We use it on top of pies, tarts and slices. Add vibrant-colored superfood powders (such as spirulina or matcha powder for green, beet powder for pink or even ground turmeric for yellow) to color the frosting naturally and add different flavors. I like to add beet powder to this and use it as a garnish on fruit desserts. We use this on top of the Strawberry Rose Pistachio Cream Slice (page 140).

In a high-speed blender, blend together the cashews, almond milk, agave, lemon juice and vanilla until smooth. Add the melted coconut oil and blend again until combined.

Transfer the frosting to a shallow container and chill in the fridge for 12 to 24 hours. Depending on your environment and fridge temperature, the setting time will vary. When the frosting is set, it should be firm to the touch. If the frosting is not set in the fridge after 24 hours, place it in the freezer for 20 to 30 minutes to firm up.

This frosting freezes well in a sealed container for a couple of months. Thaw it in the fridge for 2 days before use.

1 cup (140 g) raw cashews, soaked for 2 hours and rinsed

¼ cup (60 ml) Almond Milk (page 24)

¼ cup (85 g) light-amber agave

1 tbsp (15 ml) fresh lemon juice

6 drops vanilla extract, Medicine Flower brand preferred

½ cup (120 ml) melted virgin coconut oil

DOUBLE CHOCOLATE FROSTING

This frosting is a chocolate lover's dream and happened by accident. A high-speed blender is required to blend the cacao nibs to a smooth consistency for piping. It is a firm frosting and holds up very well. We make a mocha version of this frosting to frost the Three-Layer Tiramisu Cake (page 81) and as a garnish on top of the Chocolate Hazelnut Praline Tarts (page 105).

Yield: About 4 cups (960 ml)

In a high-speed blender, blend together the cashews, coconut nectar, water, cacao powder, cacao nibs, lemon juice and vanilla until smooth. You may require your tamper while blending this recipe, as it's thick. Add the melted coconut oil and blend again until combined.

Transfer the frosting to a shallow container and chill in the fridge for 8 to 12 hours. Depending on your environment and fridge temperature, the setting time will vary. When the frosting is set, it should be firm to the touch. This recipe freezes well in a sealed container for a couple of months. If using it from the freezer, thaw it in the fridge for 2 days before use.

1½ cups (210 g) raw cashews, soaked for 2 hours and rinsed

½ cup (120 ml) coconut nectar

¼ cup (60 ml) water

¼ cup (24 g) cacao powder

3 tbsp (22.5 g) cacao nibs

2 tbsp (30 ml) fresh lemon juice

12 drops vanilla extract, Medicine Flower brand preferred

½ cup + 2 tbsp (150 ml) melted virgin coconut oil

PRO TIP: This frosting is quite firm but holds up well at room temperature. Let it thaw at room temperature for a couple of hours before use. This batch will frost an entire 4-inch (10-cm) three-layer cake.

CULTURED CASHEW FROSTING BASE

Culture your own cashew frosting at home to create a cheesecake-flavored frosting. We use this as a base in the Carrot Cake with Orange Cheesecake Frosting (page 76). Culturing is a fermentation process whereby a microbial starter, such as probiotics, is used. Culturing the cashews is also important to help with the flavor profile used in raw desserts. Using an excellent high-speed blender for this recipe is critical as the mixture is really thick.

Yield: 2½ cups (600 ml)

Before fermenting at home, sterilize all the equipment you're using for this recipe by running them through the dishwasher on the sanitize cycle or soaking them in equal parts hot water and white vinegar in your sink and rinsing them well. Open the probiotics capsules and pour the contents into the bottom of a high-speed blender. Add the soaked cashews and filtered water, and blend until incorporated. The mixture does not need to be entirely smooth as it will be blended again in the recipes to achieve a smooth texture.

Transfer the mixture to a glass bowl and cover the top of the mixture with a piece of parchment paper. Cover the bowl with a clean tea towel and place in a warm area for 12 to 24 hours. If you do not have a warm spot in your house, place it in a microwave with its door closed. A microwave is usually much warmer than the outside ambient temperature.

The longer you leave the mixture to culture, the tangier it will taste. Feel free to taste it every 12 hours to culture to your desired taste. If the mixture has formed a crust on top, that is fine—it will be blended and incorporated. If you're not ready to make the frosting that calls for this recipe, but the cashews are tangy enough, place it in the fridge to stop the fermentation.

2 capsules dairy-free probiotics (15 billion strains or more)

2 cups (280 g) raw cashews, soaked for 2 hours and rinsed

½ cup (120 ml) filtered water

PRO TIP: This batch will frost an entire 4½-inch (11.5-cm) three-layer cake.

CANDIED CACAO NIBS

Yield: 1 cup (125 g)
Nut-free

This is a great garnish, and I love to sneak it into recipes for added texture. These are basically chocolate-covered cacao nibs, but this process makes the nibs much easier to eat and less bitter. Using a runny, thinner liquid sweetener is important for this recipe because a thicker sweetener will cause the chocolate to seize. Refer to the Troubleshooting Chocolate section (page 21) before working with chocolate.

In a stainless-steel or heatproof glass bowl, combine the cacao butter and cacao paste and gently melt them using the double boiler method (page 19), being careful not to burn the chocolate. While the bowl is still over the heat, add the coconut nectar and vanilla and stir until combined.

Remove the bowl from the heat and let the chocolate sit at room temperature for 15 minutes to cool. If you add the cacao nibs too early, they will melt. To help cool the chocolate quicker, transfer the melted chocolate to a fresh bowl. Add the cacao nibs and coconut sugar, and mix well until combined. Transfer the mixture to a lined shallow container or baking sheet and chill in the fridge for 1 hour. Transfer to a food processor and process until a crumble is formed.

This recipe will last for several months in a sealed container in the fridge.

20 g chopped cacao butter

60 g chopped cacao paste

1 tbsp (15 ml) coconut nectar

8 drops vanilla extract, Medicine Flower brand preferred

½ cup (60 g) cacao nibs

2 tbsp (20 g) coconut sugar

DARK CHOCOLATE GANACHE

Yield: About 2¼ cups (535 ml)
Nut-free

This recipe is my favorite chocolate ganache to add on top of bars and slices and to use as a drip on a cake. Be careful not to overheat your coconut oil, or it will not set properly. This recipe will melt quickly if you live in a warm climate, so I suggest adding 2 tablespoons (25 ml) of melted cacao butter to provide more stability. We use this on top of the Double Chocolate Red Velvet Brownies (page 137), Tiger Nut Tahini Slice (page 134), on the Chocolate Mousse Cake with Cherry Jam (page 67) and as a drip on the Three-Layer Tiramisu Cake (page 81).

In a blender, blend together the coconut nectar, melted coconut oil, cacao powder, vanilla and salt until smooth, approximately 30 seconds. Depending on the thickness of your sweetener, this will be difficult to blend, but once you add the water, it will thin out and blend easier. If your coconut nectar is quite thick, refer to the Substitutions List (page 160) for other options. While blending on low speed, add the room-temperature water and blend for only a few seconds until incorporated. Use immediately as instructed in the recipes.

⅔ cup (160 ml) coconut nectar

½ cup (120 ml) melted virgin coconut oil

1 cup (96 g) cacao powder

10 drops vanilla extract, Medicine Flower brand preferred

¼ tsp Himalayan salt

¼ cup (60 ml) room-temperature water

PRO TIP: This recipe makes enough for one top layer on one 8-inch (20-cm) square cake or a top layer on two 4½-inch (11.5-cm) cakes.

CHOCOLATE SAUCE

Yield: 2¼ cups (540 ml)
Nut-free

This is a wonderful addition as a garnish on dessert plates. This chocolate sauce goes well with the Banana Cream Pie with Gingerbread Crust (page 115), Chocolate Mint Cream Tarts (page 102), Mocha Crisp Cheesecake (page 64), Mexican Chocolate Mousse Bars (page 47), Mint Chocolate Chip Ice Cream (page 123), Mango Berry Crêpe with Coconut Cream (page 98) and Chocolate Mousse Cake with Cherry Jam (page 67) recipes.

In a blender, blend together the cacao powder, melted cacao butter, melted coconut oil, coconut sugar and vanilla on low to medium speed until smooth. While the blender is running on low speed, slowly add the warm water and blend for a few seconds until incorporated. Do not overblend the chocolate sauce; it will start seizing if it heats up too much.

Store at room temperature for a week or in the refrigerator for months. If stored in the fridge, it will harden and need to be melted again before use. Melt the chocolate sauce using the bowl over bowl method (page 19).

¾ cup (72 g) cacao powder

¼ cup (50 g) chopped and melted cacao butter

¼ cup (60 ml) melted virgin coconut oil

½ cup (80 g) coconut sugar

6 drops vanilla extract, Medicine Flower brand preferred

½ cup (120 ml) warm water

ENROBING DARK CHOCOLATE

Yield: About 1¼ cups (295 ml)
Nut-free

Enrobing means to coat a product with chocolate. We use this technique in quite a few recipes, including the Orange Hazelnut Fudge (page 37), White Chocolate Peppermint Fudge (page 34), Mexican Chocolate Mousse Bars (page 47) and more. This recipe is basically just dark chocolate, but the ratio of paste to butter is the perfect consistency for this technique. Making your own chocolate at home is very simple and requires only four ingredients. The key to a nice enrobing finish on chocolate is the consistency of the chocolate. The higher the ratio of paste, the thicker the chocolate. This recipe is three parts cacao paste and one part cacao butter, making it dark but also thicker in consistency, so it's easier to work with. If you like lighter, less-bitter chocolate, add more sweetener, decrease the ratio of cacao paste to butter or try equal parts (1:1).

In a stainless steel or heatproof glass bowl, combine the cacao butter and cacao paste and melt them down using the bowl over bowl method (page 19), being careful not to burn the chocolate. While the bowl is still over the heat, add the coconut nectar and vanilla and stir until combined.

Remove the bowl from the heat and let the chocolate sit at room temperature for 15 minutes to cool. If you use it while it is still hot, the recipe you're enrobing will melt. Transfer the chocolate to a small bowl for enrobing. This chocolate will last several months in a sealed container in the fridge. To remelt the chocolate, follow the instructions for the bowl over bowl method (page 19).

¼ cup (50 g) chopped cacao butter
¾ cup (150 g) chopped cacao paste
3 tbsp (45 ml) coconut nectar
12 drops vanilla extract, Medicine Flower brand preferred

PRO TIP: If your coconut nectar has a thick consistency, it will cause the chocolate to seize. To learn more about this, refer to the Trouble-shooting Chocolate section on page 21. Use pure maple syrup or agave instead. This recipe has a dark chocolate taste, which some people find to be bitter. If you want to decrease the bitterness, flavor balance by adding a little more sweetener or a pinch of salt.

VANILLA BEAN COCONUT WHIP

Yield: 2½ cups (600 ml)
Nut-free

I love the specks of vanilla bean seeds visible in this recipe; they make this whip a stunning addition to dessert plates or as frosting on a cake. When garnishing with this recipe, use a piping bag and either the recommended piping tip or your choice. If you cannot source young coconut meat, check out the Substitutions List (page 160) for more options. If not available locally, vanilla beans are easy to source on Amazon; try to get some if you can! They work so well in this recipe by adding a bold flavor and the seeds look really pretty in contrast to the coconut whip.

In a high-speed blender, blend together the coconut meat, coconut cream, xylitol, sunflower lecithin, vanilla (if using vanilla extract) and salt until smooth. Add the melted coconut oil and blend again for a few seconds until combined. If using the vanilla bean, slice it down the middle and remove the seeds with the tip of your knife by scraping the bean. Add them to the blender and blend again on low speed for a few seconds to incorporate the vanilla bean seeds.

Transfer the mixture to a container and chill it in the fridge to set for a minimum of 6 hours.

When ready to use this recipe, remove it from the fridge and check the consistency for piping. If it's too firm, allow it to soften at room temperature. This recipe keeps well in the freezer for up to 1 month or in the fridge for 3 days.

1 cup (160 g) chopped young coconut meat

½ cup (120 ml) Coconut Cream (page 27)

¼ cup (49 g) powdered xylitol (see Prep Notes on page 18)

1½ tsp (scant 4 g) sunflower lecithin powder

1 vanilla bean, or 8 drops vanilla extract, Medicine Flower brand preferred

⅛ tsp Himalayan salt

¼ cup (60 ml) melted virgin coconut oil

WHITE CHOCOLATE SAUCE

This is a fun recipe for marbling the tops of cakes, chocolates and treats. We use it to create the stunning decoration on top of the Double Chocolate Red Velvet Brownies (page 137) and the White Chocolate Peppermint Fudge (page 34) and to marble the top of the Mocha Crisp Cheesecake (page 64).

Yield: 1¼ cups (300 ml)

In a high-speed blender, blend together the cashews, water, melted cacao butter, agave and vanilla until smooth. If the mixture is difficult to blend, add 1 to 2 more tablespoons (15 to 30 ml) of water. Transfer the sauce to a squeeze bottle or piping bag for garnishing. Store the extra sauce in the fridge for up to 1 week or in the freezer for 1 month; melt before use, using the bowl over bowl method as explained on page 19.

¾ cup (105 g) raw cashews, soaked for 2 hours and rinsed

¼ cup (60 ml) water

40 g chopped cacao butter, melted

2 tbsp (43 ml) light-amber agave

6 drops vanilla extract, Medicine Flower brand preferred

GINGER CARAMEL SAUCE

This recipe is a raw vegan, rich caramel sauce without dates. This is a wonderful addition to the Vanilla Bean Ice Cream (page 120) or the Apple Crumble Caramel Cheesecake (page 58). Replace the Almond Milk (page 24) with Coconut Milk (page 27) for a nut-free version.

Yield: 1½ cups (360 ml)

In a blender, blend together the lucuma powder, almond milk, coconut nectar, coconut sugar, ginger, vanilla and salt until smooth. Add the melted coconut oil and blend for a few seconds on low until incorporated. Transfer the caramel sauce to a container and place in the fridge for 3 hours to thicken. Once the coconut oil cools, it will start thickening the sauce.

Once thickened, transfer the caramel sauce to a squeeze bottle or piping bag and use immediately or store in the fridge in a sealed container. If stored in the fridge, the mixture will need to be melted before use. Use the double boiler method (page 19) to heat the sauce over low heat. Enjoy this wonderful treat as a garnish and topping on cakes and ice creams. Store in the fridge for up to 5 days.

⅓ cup (40 g) lucuma powder

½ cup (120 ml) Almond Milk (page 24)

¼ cup + 2 tbsp (90 ml) coconut nectar

2 tbsp (20 g) coconut sugar

½ tsp grated fresh ginger

6 drops vanilla extract, Medicine Flower brand preferred

⅛ tsp Himalayan salt

¼ cup (60 ml) melted virgin coconut oil

SUBSTITUTIONS LIST

Ingredient	Substitution
Almond butter	Hazelnut butter or tahini, roasted or raw
Almond Milk (page 24)	Brazil Nut Milk (page 25)
Apples	Pears
Blackberries	Blueberries
Brazil nuts	Almonds (not interchangeable, vice versa)
Butternut squash	Sugar pumpkin
Coconut nectar	Pure maple syrup or dark-amber agave
Dried apricots	Medjool dates (keep in mind dates are much sweeter)
Dried golden figs	Medjool dates
Frozen tart cherries	Frozen berries
Hazelnut butter	Almond butter or tahini, roasted or raw
Maca powder	Mesquite powder
Matcha powder	Moringa powder (truer to color), spirulina or chlorella powder
Medicine Flower brand flavor extracts	Any extracts, preferably alcohol-free. Use 1 to 2 teaspoons per recipe to taste. 5 drops of vanilla Medicine Flower flavor extract equals 1 teaspoon of vanilla extract.
Medjool dates	Thompson or golden raisins
Mesquite powder	Maca powder or lucuma powder
Oat groats	Steel-cut oats
Orange essential oil	Orange extract
Peppermint essential oil	Mint extract
Poppy seeds	Omit
Strawberries	Raspberries
Sunflower lecithin powder	Non-GMO soy lecithin powder
Tahini	Almond butter, roasted or raw
Tiger nuts	Soaked and dehydrated almonds
Tiger nut flour	Almond flour
Vanilla beans	Any vanilla extract—½ teaspoon per ½ vanilla bean
White mulberries, dried	Thompson or golden raisins
Xylitol	Erythritol or lakanto (monk fruit)
Young coconut meat	¾ cup (105 g) of raw cashews (soaked for 2 hours and rinsed) for every 1 cup (160 g) of young coconut meat

ACKNOWLEDGMENTS

Writing this book was one of the most rewarding and challenging experiences of my life, and I could not have done it without my wonderfully supportive husband. Thank you, hubby, for emotionally supporting me through this process, taking on more house chores and making sure I had food in the fridge.

This book would not be possible without my publisher, Page Street Publishing. Thank you for giving me this opportunity and believing in me and my work—especially Franny, for always working around my busy schedule and for your continued positive encouragement.

Also, a big thank-you to my colleagues and friends who pushed and encouraged me to take on this project and did not let me quit (which seemed impossible at the time). You know who you are, and I'm so blessed to have you in my life.

Thank you to everyone who believed in me, gave me the opportunity to teach, learn alongside you and cater your retreats. I'm forever grateful for those experiences!

Lastly, all my love to the raw foodie legends who paved the way for others like me to thrive in this industry and teaching us your Jedi ways. You all have inspired us to be better. Thank you for being you.

ABOUT THE AUTHOR

Crystal Bonnet is an international raw food chef and educator. She has been traveling the world, teaching elevated raw, plant-based cuisine and has catered multiple health retreats. She taught a Raw Food Chef Certification course at the famous Yoga Barn in Ubud, Bali, and had the experience as a head chef during one full season at a popular yoga retreat center in Costa del Sol, Spain.

She has helped curate menus for local restaurants in Vancouver and even a plant-based café in Jamaica. Crystal's entrepreneur journey started when she created her raw chocolate and desserts business in Edmonton, Alberta, and then discovered a passion for teaching. She has founded an online raw food culinary school, Crystal Dawn Culinary, where she teaches students worldwide about raw, living food and desserts.

She currently resides in Vancouver, Brithish Columbia, with her husband and two dogs and continues to teach students around the world through her online custom culinary classes.

INDEX

A

Activated Oat Flour, 28

agar, 12

Agar Paste, 31

agave, 12, 16

almond butter, 12

almond pulp, 24

almonds

 about, 12, 14, 20

 Almond Fig and Cardamom Cookie Sandwiches, 95–97

 Almond Milk, 24

Apple Crumble Caramel Cheesecake, 58–60

Apples, Caramelized, 58

apricots

 Apricot Jam, 44

 Apricot Pecan Butternut Squash Cake with Coconut Cream, 73–75

 Buckwheat Crunch Chocolate Bars with Apricot Jam, 44–46

Avocado Key Lime Pies with Coconut Cream, 112–114

Avocado

 Avocado Key Lime Pies with Coconut Cream, 112-114

 Mexican Chocolate Mousse Bars, 47–49

B

Banana Cream Pies with Gingerbread Crust, 115–117

bars/slices

 Buckwheat Crunch Chocolate Bars with Apricot Jam, 44–46

 Double Chocolate Red Velvet Brownies, 137–139

 Hawaiian Sunshine Crumble Squares, 143–145

 Mexican Chocolate Mousse Bars, 47–49

 Strawberry Rose Pistachio Cream Slice, 140–142

 Tiger Nut Tahini Slice, 134–136

batters, processing, 19

beet powder, 52, 142

beets

 Double Chocolate Red Velvet Brownies, 137–139

 Raspberry Beet Mousse and Carob Tarts, 111

Berries and Cream Coconut Ice-Cream Cake, 127–129

Berry Jam, Mixed, 127

blackberries

 Berries and Cream Coconut Ice-Cream Cake, 127–129

 Blackberry Ginger Lime Zebra Cheesecake, 61–63

 Mango Berry Crêpe with Coconut Cream, 98

 Raspberry Beet Mousse and Carob Tarts, 111

blenders/blending, 13, 19

blueberries

 Berries and Cream Coconut Ice-Cream Cake, 127–129

 Lavender Berry White Chocolate Truffles, 43

bowl over bowl melting method, 19

Brazil nuts

 Brazil Nut Milk, 25

 soaking, 20

Brownies, Double Chocolate Red Velvet, 137–139

buckwheat

 about, 14

 Blond Buckwheat Crunch Base, 47

 Buckwheat Crunch Chocolate Bars with Apricot Jam, 44–46

 Sprouted and Dehydrated Buckwheat, 29

bulk suppliers, organic, 14

Butter, Coconut, 31

Butternut Squash Cake with Coconut Cream, Apricot Pecan, 73–75

C

cacao, 12, 14

cacao butter, 14, 19

Cacao Espresso Dust, 92

cacao nibs, 12, 16

 Candied Cacao Nibs, 152

 Candied Nibbed Walnuts, 137

Minted Candied Cacao Nibs, 34

cacao paste, 12, 14, 16, 19

cacao powder, 12, 16

cakes

Apricot Pecan Butternut Squash Cake with Coconut Cream, 73–75

Berries and Cream Coconut Ice-Cream Cake, 127–129

Carrot Cake with Orange Cheesecake Frosting, 76–79

Chocolate Mousse Cake with Cherry Jam, 67–68

Three-Layer Tiramisu Cake, 81–83

Tropical Lime Coconut Entremets, 69–72

See also cheesecakes

Candied Cacao Nibs, 152

Candied Nibbed Walnuts, 137

Candied Pecan Crumble, 73

Candied Pecans, 107

caramel

Apple Crumble Caramel Cheese-cake, 58–60

Ginger Caramel Sauce, 159

Caramelized Apples, 58

Caramelized Hazelnuts, 37

Cardamom Cookie Sandwiches, Almond Fig and, 95–97

Carob Tarts, Beet Mousse and, 111

Carrot Cake with Orange Cheese-cake Frosting, 76–79

cashews

about, 12, 20

Cultured Cashew Filling, 30

Cultured Cashew Frosting Base, 151

Chai-Spiced Icing, 97

cheesecakes

Apple Crumble Caramel Cheese-cake, 58–60

Blackberry Ginger Lime Zebra Cheesecake, 61–63

Mocha Crisp Cheesecake, 64

Raspberry White Chocolate Cheesecake, 55–57

Strawberry Vanilla Cheesecake, 52–54

cherries

Chocolate Mousse Cake with Cherry Jam, 67–68

Milk Chocolate Cherry Cinna-mon Truffles, 40

Tart Cherry Jam, 67

chlorella, 17

chocolate

blending, 19

Buckwheat Crunch Chocolate Bars with Apricot Jam, 44–46

Candied Cacao Nibs, 152

Chocolate Chip Ice-Cream Cookie Sandwiches, 130

Chocolate Hazelnut Praline Tarts, 105–106

Chocolate Mint Cream Tarts, 102

Chocolate Mousse Cake with Cherry Jam, 67–68

Chocolate Sauce, 154

Dark Chocolate Ganache, 153

Decadent Chocolate Ice Cream, 124

Double Chocolate Frosting, 150

Double Chocolate Red Velvet Brownies, 137–139

Enrobing Dark Chocolate, 156

Lavender Berry White Chocolate Truffles, 43

melting, 19

Mexican Chocolate Mousse Bars, 47–49

Milk Chocolate Cherry Cinna-mon Truffles, 40

Mint Chocolate Chip Ice Cream, 123

Mocha Crisp Cheesecake, 64

Mocha Donuts with Espresso Glaze, 92–94

Mocha Frosting, 81

Orange Chocolate Fudge, 37

seizing, 21

Tiger Nut Tahini Slice, 134–136

troubleshooting, 21

White Chocolate Filling, 57

White Chocolate Peppermint Fudge, 34–36

White Chocolate Sauce, 158

cinnamon, in Milk Chocolate Cherry Cinnamon Truffles, 40

coconut

about, 16

Airy Coconut Cream Whipped Topping, 115

Apricot Pecan Butternut Squash Cake with Coconut Cream, 73–75

Berries and Cream Coconut Ice-Cream Cake, 127–129

Coconut Butter, 31

Coconut Cream, 27

Coconut Frosting, 148

Coconut Milk, 27

Hawaiian Sunshine Crumble Squares, 143–145

Lemon Poppy Seed Coconut Shortbread Cookies, 86–88

Tropical Lime Coconut Entremets, 69–72

Vanilla Bean Coconut Whip, 157

coconut butter, 14, 19

coconut nectar, 16

coconut oil, 16, 19

coconut pulp, 27

coconut sugar, 16, 18

coffee

Espresso Glaze, 94

Mocha Crisp Cheesecake, 64

Mocha Donuts with Espresso Glaze, 92–94

Three-Layer Tiramisu Cake, 81–83

cookies

Almond Fig and Cardamom Cookie Sandwiches, 95–97

Chocolate Chip Ice-Cream Cookie Sandwiches, 130

Lemon Poppy Seed Coconut Shortbread Cookies, 86–88

Matcha Raspberry Linzer Cookies, 89–91

Crêpes with Coconut Cream, Mango Berry, 98

crusts, 19

crystallized sweeteners, 16

Cultured Cashew Filling, 30

Cultured Cashew Frosting Base, 151

D

Dark Chocolate Ganache, 153

Decadent Chocolate Ice Cream, 124

Dehydrated Raspberry Jam, 89

dehydrators, 13

Donuts with Espresso Glaze, Mocha, 92–94

double boiler melting method, 19

Double Chocolate Frosting, 150

Double Chocolate Red Velvet Brownies, 137–139

dried fruits, 17

E

Enrobing Dark Chocolate, 156

tips for, 20, 21

Entremets, Tropical Lime Coconut, 69–72

equipment, kitchen, 13

erythritol, 16, 18

Espresso Glaze, 94

F

figs, in Almond Fig and Cardamom Cookie Sandwiches, 95–97

flavor extracts, 17

flax/flaxseeds, 14, 18

food dehydrators, 13

food processors, 13

freeze-dried fruits, 17

frostings

Coconut Frosting, 148

Cultured Cashew Frosting Base, 151

Dark Chocolate Ganache, 153

Double Chocolate Frosting, 150

Mocha Frosting, 81

Orange Cheesecake Frosting, 76

Raspberry Frosting, 55

Rich Vanilla Cream Frosting, 149

Vanilla Bean Coconut Whip, 157

fruits, dried/freeze-dried/frozen, 17

fudge

Orange Hazelnut Fudge, 37–39

White Chocolate Peppermint Fudge, 34–36

G

Ganache, Dark Chocolate, 153

garnishes

Cacao Espresso Dust, 92

Candied Cacao Nibs, 152

Caramelized Apples, 58

Chai-Spiced Frosting, 97

Chocolate Sauce, 154

Coconut Frosting, 148

Ginger Caramel Sauce, 159

Hazelnut Praline, 105

Minted Candied Cacao Nibs, 34

Rich Vanilla Cream Frosting, 149

Vanilla Bean Coconut Whip, 157

White Chocolate Sauce, 158

ginger

Banana Cream Pies with Gingerbread Crust, 115–117

Blackberry Ginger Lime Zebra
Cheesecake, 61–63

Ginger Caramel Sauce, 159

Raspberry Ginger Filling, 57

Glaze, Espresso, 94

Glaze, White Chocolate Lime, 70

H

Hawaiian Sunshine Crumble Squares,
143–145

hazelnuts

about, 14, 20

Caramelized Hazelnuts, 37

Chocolate Hazelnut Praline Tarts,
105–106

Hazelnut Milk, 25

Orange Hazelnut Fudge, 37–39

hemp seeds, 14, 20

I

ice cream

Berries and Cream Coconut Ice-
Cream Cake, 127–129

Chocolate Chip Ice-Cream
Cookie Sandwiches,
130

Decadent Chocolate Ice Cream,
124

Mint Chocolate Chip Ice Cream,
123

Mixed Berry Ice Cream, 128

Vanilla Bean Ice Cream, 120

ice-cream makers, 13

Icing, Chai-Spiced, 97

ingredients, essential notes and tips,
12–21

J

jams/jellies

Apricot Jam, 44

Dehydrated Raspberry Jam, 89

Fig and Cardamom Jam, 97

Mango Pineapple Jelly, 69

Mixed Berry Jam, 127

Strawberry Jelly, 54

Tart Cherry Jam, 67

K

Key Lime Pies with Coconut Cream,
Avocado, 112–114

kitchen equipment/tools, 13

L

Lavender Berry White Chocolate
Truffles, 43

Lemon Poppy Seed Coconut Shortbread Cookies, 86–88

limes

Avocado Key Lime Pies with Coconut Cream, 112–114

Blackberry Ginger Lime Zebra
Cheesecake, 61–63

Tropical Lime Coconut En-
tremets, 69–72

Linzer Cookies, Matcha Raspberry,
89–91

liquefying ingredients, 19–20

M

macadamia nuts

about, 14, 20

Hawaiian Sunshine Crumble
Squares, 143–145

mango

Hawaiian Sunshine Crumble
Squares, 143–145

Mango Berry Crêpe with Coconut Cream, 98

Mango Pineapple Jelly, 69

Tropical Lime Coconut En-
tremets, 69–72

maple syrup, 16

Matcha Raspberry Linzer Cookies,
89–91

melting ingredients, 19–20

Mexican Chocolate Mousse Bars,
47–49

Milk Chocolate Cherry Cinnamon
Truffles, 40

mint

Chocolate Mint Cream Tarts, 102

Mint Chocolate Chip Ice Cream,
123

Minted Candied Cacao Nibs, 34

White Chocolate Peppermint
Fudge, 34–36

mise en place technique, 14

Mixed Berry Ice Cream, 128

Mixed Berry Jam, 127

Mocha Crisp Cheesecake, 64

Mocha Donuts with Espresso Glaze, 92–94

Mocha Frosting, 81

Mousse, Raspberry Beet, 111

Mousse Bars, Mexican Chocolate, 47–49

Mousse Cake with Cherry Jam, Chocolate, 67–68

N

nut butters, 12, 14

nuts, 14

    soaking time chart, 20

O

oats

    Activated Oat Flour, 28

    Apple Crumble Caramel Cheese-cake, 58–60

    Hawaiian Sunshine Crumble Squares, 143–145

    Spiced Walnut Oat Crumble, 58

Orange, Pecan Pie with Rosemary and, 107–108

Orange Cheesecake Frosting, Carrot Cake with, 76–79

Orange Hazelnut Fudge, 37–39

organic bulk suppliers, 14

P

pecans

    Apricot Pecan Butternut Squash Cake with Coconut Cream, 73–75

    Candied Pecan Crumble, 73

    Candied Pecans, 107

    Pecan Milk, 26

    Pecan Pie with Rosemary and Orange, 107–108

    soaking, 20

peppermint essential oil

    Chocolate Mint Cream Tarts, 102

    Mint Chocolate Chip Ice Cream, 123

    White Chocolate Peppermint Fudge, 34–36

phytic acid, 20

pies

    Avocado Key Lime Pies with Co-conut Cream, 112–114

    Banana Cream Pies with Ginger-bread Crust, 115–117

    Pecan Pie with Rosemary and Orange, 107–108

pineapple

    Hawaiian Sunshine Crumble Squares, 143–145

    Mango Pineapple Jelly, 69

    Tropical Lime Coconut En-tremets, 69–72

pistachios

    Pistachio Milk, 26

    soaking, 20

    Strawberry Rose Pistachio Cream Slice, 140–142

poppy seeds, in Lemon Poppy Seed Coconut Shortbread Cookies, 86–88

Praline, Hazelnut, 105

prepping ingredients, 18

psyllium, 18

pumpkin seeds, 14, 20

"putting in place" technique, 14

R

raspberries

    Dehydrated Raspberry Jam, 89

    Matcha Raspberry Linzer Cook-ies, 89–91

    Raspberry Beet Mousse and Carob Tarts, 111

    Raspberry White Chocolate Cheesecake, 55–57

raw desserts, defined, 12

raw desserts, ingredients in, 12–21

Red Velvet Brownies, Double Choco-late, 137–139

Rich Vanilla Cream Frosting, 149

rose extract, in Strawberry Rose Pistachio Cream Slice, 140–142

Rosemary and Orange, Pecan Pie with, 107–108

S

sauces

    Chocolate Sauce, 154

    Ginger Caramel Sauce, 159

    White Chocolate Sauce, 158

seed butters, 12

seeds, 14, 20

seized chocolate, 21

slices/bars

    Buckwheat Crunch Chocolate Bars with Apricot Jam, 44–46

    Double Chocolate Red Velvet Brownies, 137–139

    Hawaiian Sunshine Crumble Squares, 143–145

    Mexican Chocolate Mousse Bars, 47–49

    Strawberry Rose Pistachio Cream Slice, 140–142

    Tiger Nut Tahini Slice, 134–136

soaking time chart for nuts/seeds, 20

Spiced Walnut Crumble, 76

Spiced Walnut Oat Crumble, 58

spirulina, 17

Sprouted and Dehydrated Buckwheat, 29

storing ingredients, 14–17

strawberries

    Berries and Cream Coconut Ice-Cream Cake, 127–129

    Mango Berry Crêpe with Coconut Cream, 98

    Strawberry Jelly, 54

    Strawberry Rose Pistachio Cream Slice, 140–142

    Strawberry Vanilla Cheesecake, 52–54

substitutions list, 160

sugar alcohols, 16

sunflower lecithin powder, 17

sunflower seeds, 20

superfood powders, 17

suppliers, organic bulk, 14

sweeteners, 12, 16

T

tahini, 12

Tahini Slice, Tiger Nut, 134–136

Tart Cherry Jam, 67

tarts

    Chocolate Hazelnut Praline Tarts, 105–106

    Chocolate Mint Cream Tarts, 102

    Raspberry Beet Mousse and Carob Tarts, 111

techniques in raw dessert making, 19–21

Three-Layer Tiramisu Cake, 81–83

Tiger Nut Tahini Slice, 134–136

Tiramisu Cake, Three-Layer, 81–83

tools, kitchen, 13

Tropical Lime Coconut Entremets, 69–72

troubleshooting chocolate, 21

Truffles, Lavender Berry White Chocolate, 43

Truffles, Milk Chocolate Cherry Cinnamon, 40

V

vanilla

    Orange Vanilla Cream, 146

    Rich Vanilla Cream Frosting, 149

    Strawberry Vanilla Cheesecake, 52–54

    Vanilla Bean Coconut Whip, 157

    Vanilla Bean Ice Cream, 120

W

walnuts

    about, 14, 20

    Candied Nibbed Walnuts, 137

    Spiced Walnut Crumble, 76

    Spiced Walnut Oat Crumble, 58

white chocolate

    Lavender Berry White Chocolate Truffles, 43

    Raspberry White Chocolate Cheesecake, 55–57

    White Chocolate Lime Glaze, 70

    White Chocolate Orange Drizzle, 39

    White Chocolate Peppermint Fudge, 34–36

    White Chocolate Sauce, 158

X

xylitol, 16, 18